THE EVERYTHING EASY WORD SEARCH BOOK

Dear Reader,

Relax. This one is different. Most puzzle books want to twist your brain until it hurts. This book is filled with puzzles to make you feel good! Word search puzzles can do this by gently focusing our attention on a fun challenge that is never insurmountable. They give us a sea of letters, a place to lose ourselves as we find words. We return to the real world refreshed and maybe a little sharper.

I love creating word search puzzles, so it was a pleasure making this book for you. Each puzzle has a theme and I cover a variety of interesting topics. I made the puzzles easy, but not *too* easy. There are still plenty of those addictive "Aha!" moments as words are circled. Your brain will thank you for the workout.

Now sit back, relax, and engage your brain. I hope you find the journey through these pages rewarding. Enjoy!

Charles Timmerman

Welcome to the EVERYTHING® Series!

These handy, accessible books give you all you need to tackle a difficult project, gain a new hobby, comprehend a fascinating topic, prepare for an exam, or even brush up on something you learned back in school but have since forgotten.

You can choose to read an Everything® book from cover to cover or just pick out the information you want from our four useful boxes: e-questions, e-facts, e-alerts, and e-ssentials. We give you everything you need to know on the subject, but throw in a lot of fun stuff along the way, too.

We now have more than 400 Everything® books in print, spanning such wide-ranging categories as weddings, pregnancy, cooking, music instruction, foreign language, crafts, pets, New Age, and so much more. When you're done reading them all, you can finally say you know Everything®!

PUBLISHER Karen Cooper

MANAGING EDITOR, EVERYTHING® SERIES Lisa Laing

COPY CHIEF Casey Ebert

ASSISTANT PRODUCTION EDITOR Melanie Cordova

ACQUISITIONS EDITOR Lisa Laing

EDITORIAL ASSISTANT Matthew Kane

EVERYTHING® SERIES COVER DESIGNER Erin Alexander

LAYOUT DESIGNERS Erin Dawson, Michelle Roy Kelly, Elisabeth Lariviere

Visit the entire Everything® series at *www.everything.com*

THE
EVERYTHING®
EASY
WORD SEARCH
BOOK

More than 200 fun, quick word search puzzles

Charles Timmerman
Founder of Funster.com

Adams Media
New York   London   Toronto   Sydney   New Delhi

Dedicated to Suzanne, Calla, and Meryl.

Adams Media
An Imprint of Simon & Schuster, Inc.
100 Technology Center Drive
Stoughton, MA 02072

An Everything® Series Book.
Everything® and everything.com® are registered trademarks of Simon & Schuster, Inc.

ADAMS MEDIA and colophon are trademarks of Simon and Schuster.

For information about special discounts for bulk purchases, please contact Simon & Schuster Special Sales at 1-866-506-1949 or business@simonandschuster.com.

The Simon & Schuster Speakers Bureau can bring authors to your live event. For more information or to book an event contact the Simon & Schuster Speakers Bureau at 1-866-248-3049 or visit our website at www.simonspeakers.com.

Manufactured in the United States of America

17 2024

ISBN 978-1-4405-4268-8

CONTENTS

Acknowledgments

I would like to thank each and every one of the more than half a million people who have visited my website, *www.funster.com*, to play word games and puzzles. You have shown me how much fun puzzles can be and how addictive they can become!

It is a pleasure to acknowledge the folks at Adams Media who made this book possible. I particularly want to thank my editor, Lisa Laing, for so skillfully managing the many projects we have worked on together.

Introduction

THE PUZZLES IN THIS book are in the traditional word search format. Words in the list are hidden in the puzzle in any direction: up, down, forward, backward, or diagonally. The words are always found in a straight line and letters are never skipped. Words can overlap. For example, the two letters at the end of the word "MAST" could be used as the start of the word "STERN." Only uppercased letters are used, and any spaces in an entry are removed. For example, "TROPICAL FISH" would be found in the puzzle as "TROPICALFISH." Apostrophes and hyphens are also omitted in the puzzles. Draw a circle around each word that you find. Then cross the word off the list so that you will always know which words remain to be found.

A favorite strategy is to look for the first letter in a word, then see if the second letter is in any of the neighboring letters, and so on until the word is found. Or instead of searching for the first letter in a word, it is sometimes easier to look for letters that stand out, like Q, U, X, and Z. Double letters in a word will also stand out and be easier to find. Another strategy is to simply scan each row, column, and diagonal looking for any words.

PUZZLES

CHAPTER 1

ARTS & CULTURE

Musical Theater

```
R Z D U P Q G O D S P E L L
A I L N H W O R D S C A S T
D R A M A H Y I O N C T F T
X A E H N B A S E A O W H M
V T I P T L W I T R P E G U
P A S H O W D S Y A A B N S
O T H G M U A C D T G B I I
S N U S A E O U E E B E S C
O E M U E M R R M K N R C S
N L O R P U B T O C E E I O
G A R O L T C A C I I N R L
C T S H A S H I T T N T Y O
V E F C Y O E N O D N O L V
R E D E K C I W V D A N C E
```

ACT	COSTUME	LOVE	SOLO
ANNIE	CURTAIN	LYRICS	SONG
AUDIENCE	DANCE	MUSIC	STAGE
BAND	DIALOGUE	OPERA	STORY
BROADWAY	DRAMA	PHANTOM	TALENT
CAST	GODSPELL	PIT	THEATER
CATS	HAIR	PLAY	TICKET
CHORUS	HIT	RENT	WEBBER
COMEDY	HUMOR	SHOW	WICKED
COMPOSER	LONDON	SING	WORDS

Solution on page 248

Blondie Comics

```
U X A M E R I C A N H E R B
O G S L F S C L A S S I C O
L G N R E U S P H C U O C S
C P A I E X N D M O V I E S
S A I G L P A N I O X C L E
L H T R N P A N Y K C A K R
E O O E T U M P D I T R B I
E G O P R S O U S E O T U E
P O T P P I C Y D W R O T S
O D S A R I N I C Y E O H U
M A I L M A N G M I B N T N
L I E F I W C G E O H A A D
E S R E T C A R A H C C B A
W Y Z S A N D W I C H E S Y
```

ALEXANDER	CHIC YOUNG	FUNNY	NEWSPAPERS
AMERICAN	CLASSIC	GAG	SANDWICHES
BABY DUMPLING	COMIC STRIP	HERB	SERIES
BATHTUB	COOKIE	KIDS	SHOPPING
BOSS	COUCH	LATE	SLEEP
CARPOOL	DAISY	LOU	SUNDAY
CARTOON	DOG	MAILMAN	TOOTSIE
CATERING	ELMO	MOVIES	WIFE
CHARACTERS	FLAPPER GIRL	NAP	WORK

Solution on page 248

The Mona Lisa

```
Y H G E L A G I O C O N D A
D I E N F R A N C E O A T T
A S X F I I E R I I W M S O
L T P A B N W X T T E O I I
S O R M E S A I H W N W T R
R R E O N U S E E I O I R T
O Y S U M O D E L E B R A A
T W S S P I C Y O C G I K P
I U I M O R R I U A U E T I
S W O R B E Y E V F A L L C
I C N K L T P O R T R A I T
V Y A L P S I D E S D M O U
B E A U T Y T I R U C E S R
U G S F E M I N I N E F V E
```

ARTIST	FEMALE	OIL
ARTWORK	FEMININE	PAINTING
BEAUTY	FRANCE	PATRIOT
CLEANING	GALLERY	PICTURE
COMPOSITION	GUARD	PORTRAIT
DISPLAY	HISTORY	SECURITY
EXHIBIT	ICON	THE LOUVRE
EXPRESSION	LA GIOCONDA	VISITORS
EYEBROWS	LADY	WIFE
FACE	MODEL	WOMAN
FAMOUS	MYSTERIOUS	

Solution on page 248

Manga Art

```
S T O R Y D E M O C W T S R
E L T S I T R A L U P O P O
M F E I A S U K O H N K O M
U F J V A S T R O B O Y R A
L A A N O B L A C K O O T N
O N P K O N U T Z P M P S C
V T A N K I C K H E R O K E
N A N I M A T I O N O P O L
A S E R N E G C H M L T O Y
W Y S E R I E S I P I E B T
I W E B M A N G A F A K V S
A C H A R A C T E R S R K H
T A C T I O N A K I R A G U
A J R R E A D A F I L M S Q
```

ACTION	CULTURE	JAPANESE	SPORTS
AKIRA	FANTASY	KOMIKKU	STORY
ANIMATION	FICTION	MARKET	STYLE
ARTIST	FILMS	PEN	TAIWAN
ASTRO BOY	GENRE	POPULAR	TOKYOPOP
BLACK	GRAPHIC NOVELS	READ	VOLUMES
BOOKS	HERO	ROMANCE	WEBMANGA
CHARACTERS	HOKUSAI	SAILOR MOON	
COMEDY	INK	SERIES	

Solution on page 248

Arts and Crafts

```
N J E W E L R Y B B O H Z T
T E H C O R C H I L D R E N
K C I R B A F P K N I T C E
R S O I E R P A P E R N R M
S C U L P T U R E A E W E E
U I D O O W T G D E C R A V
P M E M B R O I D E R Y T O
P A Q U I L T L L L A T E M
L R R N T I E L W G F D X R
I E K R O W D A E B T E T I
E C A N V A S C S T S S I B
S Y A L C O R I G A M I L B
G L U E D E C O U P A G E O
K O O B P A R C S E N N S N
```

ART	CREATE	INK	RIBBON
BEADWORK	CROCHET	JEWELRY	SCRAPBOOK
CALLIGRAPHY	DECOUPAGE	KNIT	SCULPTURE
CANVAS	DESIGN	METAL	SEW
CERAMICS	EMBROIDERY	MOVEMENT	SUPPLIES
CHILDREN	FABRIC	NEEDLE	TAPE
CLAY	GLITTER	ORIGAMI	TEXTILES
COLOR	GLUE	PAPER	TRADITIONAL
CRAFTSMAN	HOBBY	QUILT	WOOD

Solution on page 249

American Folklore

```
V B I N O T G N I H S A W S
P E C O S B I L L E L T G Z
I S I R E J O H N H E N R Y
L A S R M C R O Y H O B B S
G T U O A S J N R S A V A U
R N M Z J Y T A O E N R U B
I O C H E R R Y T R E E N M
M H N S S D A N S I C I C U
S A A K S N D U F F D T L L
E C T O E E I B E P O N E O
L O I O J G T L I M T O S C
A P V B S E I U L A E R A B
T S E W D L O A E C S F M D
W E S T E R N P B L U E O X
```

ANECDOTES	FRONTIER	POCAHONTAS
ART	JESSE JAMES	ROY HOBBS
BABE	JOHN HENRY	SONGS
BELIEFS	LEGEND	STORY
BLUE OX	MUSIC	TALES
BOOKS	NATIVE	TRADITION
CAMPFIRE	OLD WEST	UNCLE SAM
CASEY JONES	PAUL BUNYAN	WASHINGTON
CHERRY TREE	PECOS BILL	WESTERN
COLUMBUS	PILGRIMS	ZORRO

Solution on page 249

Ancient Egyptian Hieroglyphs

```
O S I R I S B A N C I E N T
C U R S I V E S A C R E D B
I R Y S T K A E I Y V Z I O
T Y D E H C U O T R A C S O
O P U M A R T A P O E L C K
M A T E T E I C Y T M D O S
E P S H P L F I G S R B V U
D E H P I I U R E I Y K E M
C R O A R G L F B H E E R E
O U A R C I T A R E I H Y R
P T R G S O M A R G O E D I
T L A N G U A G E G O D S A
I U H H X S E M A N T I C N
C C P H O N E T I C O D E S
```

AFRICA	DEMOTIC	OSIRIS
ANCIENT	DISCOVERY	PAPYRUS
BEAUTIFUL	EGYPTIAN	PHARAOHS
BIRD	EYE	PHONETIC
BOOKS	GODS	RELIGIOUS
CARTOUCHE	GRAPHEMES	SACRED
CLEOPATRA	GREEK	SCRIPT
CODES	HIERATIC	SEMANTIC
COPTIC	HISTORY	STUDY
CULTURE	IDEOGRAM	SUMERIAN
CURSIVE	LANGUAGE	TOMB

Solution on page 249

Art in America

```
E R S R E T N I A P M P I R
L O N E W Y O R K I A O W O
Y C R E A T I V E Y T P A L
T K E D U G T I A R E S N O
S W I S D N U S R O R O S C
G E T C U I L U T T I U E U
A L N U B T O A I S A T L L
L L O L O N V L S I L H A T
L C R P N I E E T H S W D U
E A F T C A R T S B A E A R
R L O U N P R E A L I S M E
Y D L R X E X H I B I T S Z
P E K E P A C S D N A L M T
E R E L T S I H W A R H O L
```

ABSTRACT	FOLK	REALISM
ANSEL ADAMS	FRONTIER	REVOLUTION
ARTIST	GALLERY	ROCKWELL
AUDUBON	HISTORY	SCULPTURE
CALDER	LANDSCAPE	SOUTHWEST
COLOR	MATERIALS	STYLE
CREATIVE	NEW YORK	VISUAL
CULTURE	PAINTERS	WARHOL
EXHIBIT	PAINTING	WHISTLER
EXPRESSION	POP	

Solution on page 249

Dance in the United States

```
S T Z T L A W L I N E V A R
O K Y Z S G R A C E F U L B
I B L E A I C L O G G I N G
D M L O L J W M M O R P A T
U O E T F I O T P O H P I H
T D K T O V A N E W Y O R K
S E E C E B S N T C L A S S
E R N M O C O D I S C O P L
R N E O G R H R T V Z S E L
U N G C I G O N I T L A R A
T C O U N T R Y O R D A F I
L L A B S A O Y N A P M O C
U S W I N G D M U S I C R O
C T H E A T E R H Y T H M S
```

ALVIN AILEY	DISCO	MODERN	ROCK
ART	FOLK	MOTION	SOCIAL
BALL	GENE KELLY	MOVEMENT	STUDIOS
CLASS	GRACEFUL	MUSIC	SWING
CLOGGING	HIP HOP	NEW YORK	TAP
COMPANY	HISTORIC	PERFORM	TECHNO
COMPETITION	JAZZ	PROM	THEATER
COUNTRY	JIG	RAVE	TWIST
CULTURE	LEAD	RHYTHM	WALTZ
DANCERS	LINE	ROBOT	

Solution on page 250

Painting Art

```
Y B S B L D R Y B R U S H H F
R C R L A N D S C A P E L E
E A L U A R T W O R K U C N
L N I E S I O C P W I Q O G
L V G S T H R F O D L I L L
A A H D E S S E R O T N O I
G S T R M V A T T A L H R S
S T N E M G I P R A M C F H
N S O L V E N T A O M E U O
O I A M O I S T I L K T L L
S T Y L E U J V T D E E V E
S R D I L U T E D W D T S S
E A T L U C I F F I D A T A
L B I N D E R M E D I U M E
```

ADDITIVES
ARTISTS
ARTWORK
BINDER
BLUE
BRUSHSTROKES
CANVAS
COLORFUL
COOL
DIFFICULT
DILUTED

DRYBRUSH
EASEL
ENGLISH
FLUID
FRAME
GALLERY
ILLUSTRATION
LANDSCAPE
LESSONS
LIGHT
MATERIALS

MEDIUM
MOIST
PALETTE
PASTEL
PIGMENTS
PORTRAIT
RED
SOLVENT
STYLE
TECHNIQUES
WET

Solution on page 250

Sculpture

```
C S T D G C E P E M R O F W
B U S T L G D P D E M T O A
S O A X A I A H L Z O O M X
G M C M S H Y I O N D B J E
T A I P S F E M M O E A N V
A F L G O F U D W R L O P T
C A T L M S K U E B T F E C
Y L N S E G E T L S I C R A
Q S A U T R S N D R I T S R
S S M Y A A Y X I X I G O T
L A U A L N T N N D R V N S
O R H P R I G U G W O N S B
O B J E C T U S E V N R M A
T D T C R E A T E R U G I F
```

ABSTRACT	DISPLAY	IMAGE	RELIEF
AMBER	FAMOUS	IRON	RODIN
ART	FIGURE	METAL	SHAPE
BRASS	FIRING	MODEL	SNOW
BRONZE	FORM	MOLD	STATUE
BUST	GALLERY	MUSEUM	STONE
CAST	GLASS	OBJECT	TOOLS
CLAY	GRANITE	PERSON	WAX
CREATE	HUMAN	PLASTER	WELDING
DESIGN	ICE	POSE	WOOD

Solution on page 250

Hey, It's the Monkees!

```
Q T V S E R I E S T I H R G
K R O T R E T E P Y S S N R
H T I M S E N E K I M A T O
R G S G N O S C L I C T E U
E U L T J I O G C I V R E P
C I V Y N R N K R S D E N O
O T V G P E Y E H Y A C A P
R A E O R D M O A U E N G U
D R P U O A W U I G H O E L
S E L L I V S K R A L C R A
D N E T H E B E A T L E S R
K N A S E L E G N A S O L U
Z U A F M U S I C I A N S O
P F L B H S I T I R B X I F
```

AMERICAN
BAND
BRITISH
CLARKSVILLE
CONCERT
DAVY JONES
ENGLISH
FANS
FOUR
FUN
GROUP

GUITAR
GUYS
HAIR
HEAD
HITS
INSTRUMENTS
LOS ANGELES
MICKY DOLENZ
MIKE NESMITH
MUSICIANS
PETER TORK

POP ROCK
POPULAR
RECORDS
SINGERS
SONGS
TEENAGERS
THE BEATLES
TV SERIES
TV SHOW

Solution on page 250

Tom Sawyer

```
G W H I T E W A S H T O W N
J L T S E R U T N E V D A I
U A M U L L E B E T N A U A
D I M I G O L D M U F J N W
G R U B S R E T E P T S T T
E T F F O C R A L U P O P K
T I F U U D H E C N E F O R
H N P N T N V I L E V O L A
A J O E H A R P E R B Y L M
T U T R C L G X U V A C Y E
C N T A H S V R M B O Y S R
H J E L C I S S A L C U Z I
E O R R E Y W A S M O T S C
R E H C T A H T Y K C E B A
```

ADVENTURES

AMERICA

ANTEBELLUM

AUNT POLLY

BECKY THATCHER

BOOK

BOYS

CAVE

CLASSIC

FENCE

FUNERAL

GOLD

INJUN JOE

ISLAND

JOE HARPER

JUDGE THATCHER

LOVE

MARK TWAIN

MISCHIEVOUS

MUFF POTTER

POPULAR

SAMUEL CLEMENS

SOUTH

ST PETERSBURG

TOM SAWYER

TOWN

TRIAL

WHITEWASH

Solution on page 251

Mime Artists

```
I G P U E K A M S T R E E T
P E R F O R M C U S T A G E E
I S W U C M E P O R M L I F
B T O N H P O F I M O L R E
H U H N A S H V R V I M E C
A R S Y P R K Y E E I C T N
N E I K L E E S S M N G A A
D M L E I D E T I I E C E D
T M L A N N R N Q M C N H Q
R U U T W E G X U O S A T M
A M S O O P N O I T O M L U
B A I N L S I L E N T C A S
O S O X C U R O T A T I M I
X K N O I S S E R P X E M C
```

ACT	FILM	MAKEUP	QUIET
ART	FRENCH	MASK	ROPE
BIP	FUNNY	MIMING	SERIOUS
BOX	GESTURE	MOTION	SHOW
BUSKING	GLOVES	MOVEMENT	SILENT
CHAPLIN	GREEK	MUMMER	STAGE
CLOWN	HAND	MUSIC	STREET
COMIC	ILLUSION	PANTOMIME	SUSPENDERS
DANCE	IMITATOR	PERFORM	THEATER
EXPRESSION	KEATON	PHYSICAL	

Solution on page 251

Culture

```
U Y M Q C S O C I A L F T E
M L O Y O N P U O R G O N C
G I T R N O S I D O O F A A
N M S O C I L S E L E O T R
O A U T E T A I A I R L I E
S F C S P C O N L N C K O G
H E R I T A G E E I L R N I
O L C H R U B R S C O I M O
L P Q N A E D U T I T T A N
I O E G A L M A V N H U N A
D E E R I D S A I H I A N M
A P N H A T H A I T N L E U
Y R C V E E P G N E G S R H
S S T I B A H V A L U E S C
```

ACTIONS	CUSTOM	HIGH	PEOPLE
AMERICAN	DANCE	HISTORY	RACE
ART	ETHNIC	HOLIDAYS	REGION
ATTITUDE	FAMILY	HUMAN	RITUALS
BEHAVIOR	FOLK	LANGUAGE	SOCIAL
BELIEF	FOOD	MANNERS	SONG
CHILDREN	GOALS	MUSIC	TASTE
CLOTHING	GROUP	NATION	VALUES
CONCEPT	HABITS	OPERA	
CUISINE	HERITAGE	PAINTING	

Solution on page 251

CHAPTER 2

GOING PLACES

New York City Subway

```
R F M H S N E E U Q L I N E
A S H U T T L E S A F E T Y
I C I T Y O A I T R A C K A
L H J G K V O T G U I D B W
S E R A F R C B I H M A S B
C D D E D W O R C O T M T U
P U I R E C N Y L R N S O S
E L P O E P D O W T M E P C
P E A U P T U N N E L X C B
U O R T S D C A R M N P O R
B H L E F I T I F F A R G O
L E D I R O O D R I V E R N
I L S E C U R I T Y S S Z X
C D T O K E N M A P S S A P
```

BOOTH	FARE	PLATFORM	SECURITY
BRONX	GRAFFITI	POLICE	SHUTTLES
CAR	LIGHTS	PUBLIC	SPEED
CITY	LINE	QUEENS	STAIRS
COMMUTE	LOUD	RAILS	STATION
CONDUCTOR	MAP	RAPID	STOP
CROWDED	METRO	RIDE	SUBWAY
DOOR	NEW YORK	ROUTE	TOKEN
DRIVER	PASS	SAFETY	TRACK
EXPRESS	PEOPLE	SCHEDULE	TUNNEL

Solution on page 251

Flying the Concorde

```
H C N E R F O L G N A U U N
D Y I E C E S E N I G N E O
D E L T P N N I E S I O S M
S S U O N G A X R T S I O E
P O R N L A P R E A K T N N
E U V A I E L D F F P A P C
E N N I N T S T J R L I O L
D D L S E T N K A P I V O A
N O I T A T R O P S N A R T
T V S T H O U A C C N V D U
E A E S Y Z V N V S A A Z R
F S A W I N G S I E I B R E
U R E N I L R I A O L D I T
C N F X M O O B C I N O S N
```

AIR FRANCE	ENGLAND	SOUND
AIRLINER	EUROPE	SOVIET UNION
ANGLO FRENCH	EXPENSIVE	SPEED
AVIATION	FAST	SST
CABIN	NEW YORK JFK	TRANSATLANTIC
CRASH	NOMENCLATURE	TRANSPORTATION
DISCONTINUED	PARIS	TRAVEL
DROOP NOSE	PLANE	UNITED STATES
ENGINES	SONIC BOOM	WINGS

Solution on page 252

Traveling in Space

```
C H D E N N A M I N I M E G
W O O A T E I V O S Y M L E
K M S U H S O L L O P A T C
I A R M S T R O N G N R T N
N R T I O T U O Y D H G U E
T S O I Y N O A I A A O H I
U N T Q U M A N N J D R S C
P C R M Z S G U Y O I P R S
S S A T E L L I T E R Y E T
A S I P I R E P I L O T T E
N P N Z S B C V V R L E S N
I A I S S U R U A V F F O A
H C N U A L L O R R W A O L
C E G H T R A E G Y T S B P
```

APOLLO	GEMINI	MOON	SCIENCE
ARMSTRONG	GRAVITY	NASA	SHUTTLE
ASTRONAUT	HOUSTON	ORBIT	SOVIET
BOOSTERS	LANDING	PILOT	SOYUZ
CAPSULE	LAUNCH	PLANETS	SPACE
CHINA	MANNED	PROGRAM	SPUTNIK
COSMONAUT	MARS	RUSSIA	SUIT
EARTH	MERCURY	SAFETY	TRAINING
FLORIDA	MISSION	SATELLITE	TRAVEL

Solution on page 252

Seaplane

```
P U R A L A K E U C S E R N
L I T R O P S N A R T M I E
A T L G Z K O T V C C Y V V
A S R O Y O A L I H S C E A
K A W K T M E L A G E N R W
C O F N A R T R T N A A E R
O C O R N M T I I I D Y T C
D P A W D E P G O W T O A U
W N V P R I N H N R I U W R
A C O M M E R C I A L B D R
K T F S T S M B L B O A T E
E I H U L L M O Y M I N A N
X I O L E V A R T H Y A R T
P R F L Y V A N A E C O N P
```

AIR	COAST	LAND	SEA
ALTITUDE	COMMERCIAL	NAVY	SHIP
AMPHIBIAN	CURRENT	OCEAN	SKY
AVIATION	DOCK	PILOT	TRANSPORT
BOAT	ENGINE	PONTOON	TRAVEL
BUOYANCY	FLY	REMOTE	WAKE
CARGO	HULL	RESCUE	WATER
CATAMARAN	HYBRID	RIVER	WAVE
CHARTER	LAKE	ROUTE	WING

Solution on page 252

Around the Middle East

```
M T P Y G E Y T R E S E D J
E P A L E S T I N E M E Y U
D I R A T S I B A G H D A D
I D F L U G N A I S R E P A
T A C I R F A H T R O N M I
E M N K I J I D Z N Q A J S
R A I U E O T U G A N M E M
R S L W B R S B T A O O R B
A C E A U D I A M R Z N U A
N U A I B A R A I D U A S H
E S R T P N H A L L A M A R
A J S U E Z C A N A L M L A
N L I O E D U R C G Y A E I
Q A R I P E T R O L E U M N
```

ABU DHABI	EGYPT	NORTH AFRICA
AMMAN	GAZA	OMAN
ARID	IRAQ	PALESTINE
BAGHDAD	ISRAEL	PERSIAN GULF
BAHRAIN	JERUSALEM	PETROLEUM
BEIRUT	JORDAN	QATAR
CAIRO	JUDAISM	RAMALLAH
CHRISTIANITY	KUWAIT	SAUDI ARABIA
CRUDE OIL	MANAMA	SUEZ CANAL
DAMASCUS	MEDITERRANEAN	UAE
DESERT	NILE	YEMEN

Solution on page 252

On the Highway

```
M I C P L A N E K I P J D J
A T R U C K S A U T O E T F
P O H L D I Y A E U E R R F
I R L G O S S E R P X E A R
R O G N I P T N S T E S V C
T U N D H L E P S W T Y E I
D T O A S Y M P A V E D L P
S E L O I A T Y P T A P E S
M T D R R D G L Y S R C C N
B U S I B D E E B T I O I G
X M S U V R X M Y N I A L I
N M E G D I R B E V U C O S
L O Z L T V D C I L B U P J
N C Q S M E S T R E E T X J
```

ASPHALT	EXITS	MEDIAN	SCENIC
AUTO	EXPRESS	NOISE	SIGNS
BRIDGE	FAST	PATROL	SPEED
BUS	FREEWAY	PAVED	STREET
BYPASS	GAS	PIKE	SUV
CAR	JOURNEY	POLICE	SYSTEM
CITY	LANE	PUBLIC	TOLL
COMMUTE	LIGHT	RAMPS	TRAVEL
DIVIDED	LONG	ROAD	TRIP
DRIVE	MAP	ROUTE	TRUCKS

Solution on page 253

Antarctica Tour

```
A R C T I C G L A C I E R S
M H O S R K N E S A B F E P
E T N N E N I E N K R I L L
L R T I T O Z X I C Z S O N
T A I U A I E P A L I H P A
I E N G W T E L T I C I H T
N S E N V I R O N M E N T U
G T N E J D F R U A S G U R
R A T P S E N A O T H P O E
E T I H W P Q T M E E H S V
B I B F R X G I I S L A N D
E O Z O N E Z O R F F T O L
C N S T S I T N E I C S W O
I S O L A T E D E S E R T C
```

ARCTIC	FREEZING	NATURE
BASE	FROZEN	OZONE
CLIMATE	GLACIERS	PENGUINS
COLD	HAT	ROSS
CONTINENT	ICE SHELF	SCIENTISTS
DESERT	ICEBERG	SNOW
EARTH	ISLAND	SOUTH POLE
ENVIRONMENT	ISOLATED	STATIONS
EXPEDITION	KRILL	WATER
EXPLORATION	MELTING	WHITE
FISHING	MOUNTAINS	

Solution on page 253

Airport Letters

```
I Y F P A E O Y G R M C M F
Y A B X Y A I X T O Z U C M
L F T C S T L L F N R B O S
L Y I A G V C M T I N D K H
S S V W G W P E W A C D F W
X D G E E W D M F I G I J Y
M M K C D C X I X Y P C R K
Y K W L V G H W A U E J N G
H H R D D N P B L D B O O S
A U Z F G S I O U U P L O U
T U O R H G T E M R G B C E
W R R Z B C G L K A H N L Y
L B G Q S P P G A M S Y S N
W I O E V I C K O F S J C D
```

ATL	DET	MCO	PDX
BGR	DFW	MDW	PHX
BHM	FLL	MEM	PIT
BNA	HNL	MKE	RIC
BOS	HOU	MSY	RNO
BUR	IAD	OAK	SFO
BWI	IND	OGG	SJC
CLT	JFK	OKC	SLC
CVG	LAX	OMA	SMF
DCA	LGA	ORD	STL

Solution on page 253

Orienteering

```
Q S R Y N U F O O T I M E M
S S E A O D F E R O C S A G
C G N L C C N O R T H P A P
L A G E U E O A R E T R Q S
O L N R X R P U L E N I X D
C F I O Y E H W R I S N L O
K D N C E R R R A S W T I O
K E N O I T A C O L E E A W
S E U M F I E T I U K K R E
A P R P N A A P I S G I T M
K S T A M C M C M L E H N A
L K S S E N T I F O I Q E G
E I O S Q S B U L C C M V Z
T E L S P O R T B Y M A E T
```

CANOE	FLAGS	MAP	SPEED
CLOCK	FOOT	MILITARY	SPORT
CLUBS	FOREST	NORTH	SPRINT
COMPASS	FUN	RACE	TEAM
COMPETE	GAME	RELAY	TERRAIN
COURSE	GPS	ROUGH	TIME
EVENT	HIKE	RULES	TRAIL
EXERCISE	LAND	RUNNING	WALKING
FAMILY	LOCATION	SCORE	WINNER
FITNESS	LOST	SKI	WOODS

Solution on page 253

See India

```
I Y R O T S I H D D U B J G
E P T H I N D U I S M S D A
R N O A D O O W Y L L O B D
U O U S H I M A L A Y A S Y
T I R I B T H S T R O S E R
N G I A S C E L E P H A N T
E I S L L A F R E T A W I S
V L T S A R N A I D N I R U
D E S E V T I S I V W T H D
A R C H I T E C T U R E S N
N A A C T A J M A H A L N I
C H V A S H O P P I N G P R
E I E E E P A C S D N A L A
J B S B F C O U N T R Y N S
```

ADVENTURE	DANCE	RELIGION
ARCHITECTURE	ELEPHANT	RESORTS
ASIA	FESTIVALS	SARI
ATTRACTIONS	HIMALAYAS	SEA
BEACHES	HINDUISM	SHOPPING
BIHAR	HISTORY	SHRINES
BOLLYWOOD	INDIAN	TAJ MAHAL
BUDDHIST	INDUSTRY	TOURISTS
CAVES	LANDSCAPE	VISIT
COUNTRY	NEW DELHI	WATERFALLS

Solution on page 254

Cities of Europe

```
X L R T S E R A H C U B K B
L E H A N N O V E R A L I E
E E G M T N E M E R B K B R
I D C S R A E H C I N U M L
P S G T U N L E T I D N D I
Z U R E F Z L V S A U O N N
I I U R K O I L P A B B U E
G N B D N P E E A I L S M D
N L M A A H S M L C I I T S
E I A M R T R A E N N L R E
S V H S F M A D R E T T O R
S I R I G A M R M L Q X D D
E N G O L O C I O A O N E G
W A L C O R W D S V E M O R
```

AMSTERDAM	ESSEN	MARSEILLE
ATHENS	FRANKFURT	MUNICH
BARCELONA	GENOA	PALERMO
BERLIN	GLASGOW	POZNAN
BREMEN	HAMBURG	RIGA
BUCHAREST	HANNOVER	ROME
BUDAPEST	HELSINKI	ROTTERDAM
COLOGNE	LEEDS	VALENCIA
DORTMUND	LEIPZIG	VILNIUS
DRESDEN	LISBON	WROCLAW
DUBLIN	MADRID	

Solution on page 254

Take the Bus

```
U L Y P H P I R T R O H S G
D R O T O M K S C H O O L N
R T R U C K O C I L B U P O
U E T U M M O C S T X C T L
O J E A N V H T T U L I E E
T L M I P A A S R E T V R F
A E B B R T O Y E A A A B Z
E U C T I I E H E R F S Q L
S F E O V C W G T Z S F E T
I R N S A K O T R A N S I T
E N G G T E R A P A E R P C
D R I V E T A G C I L O R I
I B N M L R O A D H T O H T
R Y E L L O W S L S L D E Y
```

BIG	FUEL	PRIVATE	STREET
CHARTER	GAS	PUBLIC	TICKET
CITY	LARGE	RIDE	TOUR
COACH	LONG	ROAD	TRAFFIC
COMMUTE	LUXURY	ROUTE	TRANSIT
DIESEL	METRO	SCHOOL	TRAVEL
DOORS	MINI	SEAT	TRIP
DRIVE	MOTOR	SHORT	TRUCK
ENGINE	OMNIBUS	STATION	WHEEL
FARE	PASS	STOP	YELLOW

Solution on page 254

Visit Sri Lanka

```
T A P R O B A N E H O T C L
N A E C O N A I D N I R O A
O N M S I U D N I H K O F C
I A T I A R T S K L A P F I
G R C O L O M B O D F L E P
I C O U N T R Y T E F A E O
L B U D D H I S T M I N L R
E E R U P E E G E O R T E T
R A E T N O L Y E C S A P N
U C B B U R G H E R S T H E
T H B X S O U T H A S I A I
L E U C O C O N U T S O N C
U S R R A W L I V I C N T N
C D N O M A N N I C V S S A
```

ANCIENT	CULTURE	RANA
BEACHES	DEMOCRATIC	RELIGION
BUDDHIST	ELEPHANTS	RUBBER
BURGHERS	HINDUISM	RUPEE
CEYLON TEA	HOT	SEA
CINNAMON	INDIAN OCEAN	SOUTH ASIA
CIVIL WAR	KAFFIRS	TAMIL TIGERS
COCONUTS	KOTTE	TAPROBANE
COFFEE	PALK STRAIT	TROPICAL
COLOMBO	PLANTATIONS	
COUNTRY	PORT	

Solution on page 254

Aboard the Orient Express

```
H C A O C G N I P E E L S T
R I C H L L U B N A T S I R
S U O M A F M Y S T E R Y A
A T H E N S L S I R A P H N
H I S T O R Y E P E D G R S
Y A W L I A R X V Z V R A P
K O O B T C E D L O E U I O
T E C N A T S I D G N O L R
S R E G N E S S A P T B R T
I V J E R O U T E S U S O I
R S I L E U R O P E R A A C
U R H S T R M U R D E R D K
O V E R N I G H T C I T Y E
T E U G I R T N I A I S A T
```

ADVENTURE	INTRIGUE	PASSENGERS
ASIA	ISTANBUL	RAILROAD
ATHENS	LONG DISTANCE	RAILWAY
BOOK	MURDER	RICH
CARS	MYSTERY	ROUTES
CITY	NOVEL	SLEEPING COACH
EUROPE	OLD	STRASBOURG
FAMOUS	ORIENT EXPRESS	TICKET
HISTORY	OVERNIGHT	TOURIST
INTERNATIONAL	PARIS	TRANSPORT

Solution on page 255

Costa Rica Trip

```
T S N D R S R Y C I T I E S
O A A O I E E T A U R G A P
W N C O C O S I S L A N D A
N J I F H N T S N A V I V M
S O R J C A A R I N E L E V
T S A L O C U E A G L E N A
S E T A A L R V T U I K T C
I H S C S O A I N A N R U A
R C O I T V N D U G G O R T
U A C P D Q T O O E O N E I
O E R O P A S I M C B S V O
T B W R E I R B E R U T A N
S L E T O H N A N I M A L S
S W I M M I N G P E O P L E
```

ADVENTURE	MAPS	SNORKELING
ANIMALS	MOUNTAINS	SWIMMING
BEACHES	NATURE	TOURISTS
BIODIVERSITY	OCEAN	TOWNS
CITIES	PARADISE	TRAVELING
COCOS ISLAND	PEOPLE	TROPICAL
COSTA RICA	RESTAURANTS	VACATION
FOOD	RICH COAST	VOLCANOES
HOTELS	SAN JOSE	
LANGUAGE	SHOPPING	

Solution on page 255

PERSONAL ITEMS

Pocket Watch

```
S E U Q I T N A C Y O M M E
L R T E E R E V L I S H S M
E E A K C O L C A A T A O C
W L C E K W U L S E C O N D
E A O A G L A T S Y R C W R
J L P T F T C T I L E P A L
D B E E I N P O C K E T D E
E C N G T Q D N A H R Z Y A
L A I D B U G H S C O V E R
U D P A A N N T Z U G L B
M N E G H R I I E R N S Y O
D I L U O T R A M I D U T F
D W E A U Z P H H S W I S S
N L P A R T S C V E S T F V
```

ANTIQUE	DIGITAL	LAPEL	SILVER
BEZEL	FACE	LEPINE	SPRING
CASE	FOB	LID	STEM
CHAIN	GADGET	MINUTE	STRAP
CLASSIC	GEARS	OLD	STYLE
CLOCK	HAND	OPEN	SUIT
COAT	HINGE	POCKET	SWISS
COVER	HOUR	QUARTZ	VEST
CRYSTAL	JACKET	ROUND	WATCH
DIAL	JEWELS	SECOND	WIND

Solution on page 255

Necklaces

```
J H C S U S L T U C R U B Y
E I T E L U M A R L O N G R
L E N G I F T O T A M R L E
Y F A O N Z P D A E B L A V
T O D L D E S I G N M E S L
S R N D I T L J W Y G W S I
E M E R A L D O S L L E H S
T A P E M P M S K L F J J C
T L S K O E E M A A L I N K
I R A O N R H U S H O R T U
N I L H D V S H X Y C N A F
G N C C H A I N L G K C E N
V G B T C O S T U M E K W A
U J H A N G W E N O T S B S
```

AMULET	DIAMOND	HANG	RING
ART	DRESSY	JEWEL	ROPE
BEAD	EMERALD	LENGTH	RUBY
CASUAL	FANCY	LINK	SETTING
CHAIN	FASHION	LOCKET	SHELLS
CHOKER	FORMAL	LONG	SHORT
CLASP	GEM	LOOP	SILVER
CORAL	GIFT	METAL	STONE
COSTUME	GLASS	NECK	STYLE
DESIGN	GOLD	PENDANT	WOMEN

Solution on page 255

My Rolex

```
F O O R P R E T A W D I A L
W M E D E E A H S H A L N O
A E C N K T E C L O N D O N
C L A A R S S T O E R I I G
C T F L E Y P A B X E N T E
E S V R T O E W M P N N A V
S U A E E H E Z Y L I O T I
S J L Z M D D T S O R V U S
O E U T O E D R I R A A P N
R T A I N S N A L E M T E E
I A B W O I A U V R B I R P
E D L S R G R Q E I U O W X
S N E M H N B R R X S N O E
K C O L C M I L G A U S S W
```

ACCESSORIES	EXPLORER	QUARTZ WATCH
ALFRED DAVIS	FACE	REPUTATION
BRAND	FAKE	SILVER
CHRONOMETER	GOLD	SUBMARINER
CLOCK	INNOVATION	SWITZERLAND
DATEJUST	LONDON	SYMBOLS
DEEPSEA	MENS	VALUABLE
DESIGN	MILGAUSS	WATERPROOF
DIAL	OYSTER	WEALTH
EXPENSIVE	PEARLMASTER	

Solution on page 256

Sleeping Bag

```
L K I D S C G A B B S J A K
I N Q S O F T E T K F H O T
N O R T L W K C A S P A N L
I L A D V E N T U R E E W L
N Y T O U T D O O R T R O I
G N I K I H D T D E D L O F
M A N O V Z E J K R O O L F
R L G H I C T N M U M M Y N
A A S P T M A T T R E S S I
W M X I J L L O R C A M P G
B R V L B C U S H I O N A H
P E E L S S S E L E V A R T
A H D O Q D N U O R G L T I
D T W W L A I R E T A M S I
```

ADVENTURE	FOLDED	MUMMY	SACK
BAG	FOREST	NAP	SLEEP
BED	GEAR	NIGHT	SOFT
BLANKET	GROUND	NYLON	STRAPS
CAMP	HIKING	OUTDOOR	TENT
COT	INSULATED	PAD	THERMAL
CUSHION	KIDS	PILLOW	TRAVEL
DOWN	LINING	PROTECTIVE	WARM
FILL	MATERIAL	RATINGS	WOOL
FLOOR	MATTRESS	ROLL	ZIP

Solution on page 256

Personal Hygiene

```
T O I L E T P A P E R R J A
T H A N D W A S H I N G N N
O R J O B L E A C H O T C T
O P M O O R H T A B I L L I
T R T P D A I L Y P T G E B
H E S M Y S T A E S C N A I
B V I A H O W R H A E I N O
R E T H Y A S E M F F H L T
U N N S G P C W A E N T I I
S T E R I L I Z A T I O N C
H I D R E W O H S Y S L E S
W O A G N I H T A B I C S K
V N C L E A N I N G D A S I
T Y G O L O I M E D I P E N
```

ANTIBIOTICS	DAILY	SHAMPOO
ANTIPERSPIRANT	DENTIST	SHOWER
BATHING	DISINFECTION	SKIN
BATHROOM	EPIDEMIOLOGY	SOAP
BLEACH	HAIR	STERILIZATION
BODY HYGIENE	HAND WASHING	SWEAT
CLEANING	ORAL	TOILET PAPER
CLEANLINESS	PREVENTION	TOOTHBRUSH
CLOTHING	SAFETY	

Solution on page 256

Put on a Coat

```
J J D B L W G D H I I K S I
F Z E P R E V O T E E T N W
I L N A T R V O G G Y K O P
T C I R B A F E N L A O W T
E N L K J E O I E O L F I S
L D E A U W N C L L F U L L
A I I Z R R E C K A S R A I
H N R S O E M N S C H E M A
O N T M T T T H L P O S R T
O A E W E U I A C O O R O R
D B K K G O O G E N N R F O
F L C Y N U M R A W E G T H
E A O D E X U T O T S R F S
J B P C W I N D P S P O T U
```

BELT	HEM	OUTSIDE	STYLE
CLOAK	HOOD	OVER	SUIT
COLD	JACKET	PARKA	SWEATER
DOWN	LAB	POCKET	TAILS
FABRIC	LENGTH	RAIN	TOP
FASHION	LINED	SHORT	TRENCH
FIT	LONG	SKI	TUXEDO
FORMAL	MEN	SLEEVE	WARM
FROCK COAT	MORNING	SNOW	WIND
FUR	OUTERWEAR	SPORTS	WOOL

Solution on page 256

Our Eyes

```
J S D O R O N S D I L G E P
Z Z H U M A N P U P I L Y S
H Y G K G U L J D C G M A F
T S R R S D D U K O O L D C
I A O C O N T A C T P F P N
D J U Y T I U C A O T A R A
A P N Y H L T N O E I L E O
E V D E G B A H S R C X T U
H I Z W I L N T G O N L I Q
S S S H L U I F L I E E N T
A I I I S E A O V N R X A I
L O R T D C R L S I V B A I
G N I E E S B E G R E E N M
H T T H G I S E N S E W J G
```

ACUITY	DARK	LIDS	RODS
ANATOMY	EXAM	LIGHT	ROUND
BLIND	FACE	LOOK	SEEING
BLUE	FOCUS	OCULAR	SENSE
BRAIN	GREEN	OGLE	SIGHT
BRIGHT	HEAD	OPTIC NERVE	SUN
COLORS	HUMAN	ORGAN	TEST
CONTACT	IRIS	PAIR	VIEW
CORNEA	LASH	PUPIL	VISION
CRY	LENSES	RETINA	WHITE

Solution on page 257

Things to Wear

```
L W A H S S E R D Y T R A P
B O W S K P S E R R S I S A
P O N C T A E D E L T N A J
U D O G I C B V S E A G S A
E S H T U G O E S W H S H M
K M T F S N R L S E I F E A
A J S A W I D V H J G E S S
M A F N O K S E I N H I E E
I C F C N C N T R E H T L V
T K U Y S O W Q T W E K F O
T E M X U T O C S A E C F L
E T R I K S G N O L L A U G
N S A S L I P P E R S L R J
S R E T A E W S L L E B T K
```

ASCOT	GLOVES	MITTENS	SHAWL
BELLS	GOWNS	NEW	SLIPPERS
BLACK TIE	HATS	PAJAMAS	SNOWSUIT
BOOTS	HIGH HEELS	PARTY DRESS	SOCKS
BOWS	JACKETS	RED VELVET	STOCKING CAP
COATS	JEWELRY	RINGS	SWEATERS
DRESS SHIRTS	LONG SKIRT	ROBES	TUX
EARMUFFS	LONG UNDERWEAR	RUFFLES	
FANCY	MAKEUP	SASHES	

Solution on page 257

Sachet

```
R S S G L D P S L A T E P A
O N M Y E A R O M A E D E L
S E A L X L L E M S S R R L
E N L C R A F T S A T I F I
P I L L O W H O P S N E U N
F L H O M E M A D E E D M A
P O T P O U R R I W I R E V
S T N E M R A G R E D N U R
T H E R B O R E D N E V A L
U T S F B C F R A G R A N T
F O O P E N U T M E G A B N
F L U D I N O M A N N I C E
E C A L O C C U S H I O N C
D R A W E R E W O L F T K S
```

AROMA	DRESSER	LACE	POTPOURRI
BAG	DRIED	LAVENDER	ROSE
CEDAR	FILLED	LINENS	SCENT
CINNAMON	FLOWER	NUTMEG	SMALL
CLOTH	FRAGRANT	ODOR	SMELL
CRAFTS	HERB	PERFUME	SPICE
CUPBOARDS	HOMEMADE	PETALS	STUFFED
CUSHION	HOPS	PILLOW	UNDERGARMENTS
DRAWER	INGREDIENTS	POMANDER	VANILLA

Solution on page 257

Leaving Fingerprints

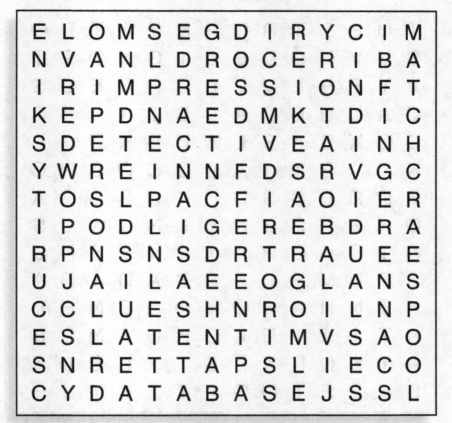

```
E L O M S E G D I R Y C I M
N V A N L D R O C E R I B A
I R I M P R E S S I O N F T
K E P D N A E D M K T D I C
S D E T E C T I V E A I N H
Y W R E I N N F D S R V G C
T O S L P A C F I A O I E R
I P O D L I G E R E B D R A
R P N S N S D R T R A U E E
U J A I L A E E O G L A N S
C C L U E S H N R O I L N P
E S L A T E N T I M V S A O
S N R E T T A P S L I E C O
C Y D A T A B A S E J S S L
```

ARRESTED	EPIDERMIS	JAIL	PERSONAL
CLUE	EVIDENCE	LABORATORY	POLICE
CRIMINALS	FBI	LATENT	POWDER
CSI	FINGER	LINES	RECORD
DATABASE	GREASE	LOOPS	RIDGES
DETECTIVE	GROOVES	MARK	SCANNER
DIFFERENT	HANDS	MATCH	SEARCH
DIRT	IMPRESSION	OIL	SECURITY
DNA	INDIVIDUAL	PATTERNS	SKIN

Solution on page 257

Your Shoes

```
T U B S T R O P S Z W T B O
B V V R C D E S I G N O F T
V Y E R L V E L C R O E O S
C A U U E C A L B T A L F D
D O K B A F L W U B K Z G B
K D V B T J A P C C O C R C
R D R E S S D O K A S C O A
O X Z R R B N L L N U W U S
W I O H C R A I E V E S N U
S P U M P L S S S A D I D A
A T N R A H O H O S E N H L
K T I A I E L G K D A N C E
A I K N R K E S T Y L E A E
D F E E T O O F T Z X T J H
```

ADIDAS	DANCE	LOAFER	SOLE
ARCH	DESIGN	NIKE	SPORTS
BOOT	DRESS	PAIR	STYLE
BUCKLES	FEET	POLISH	SUEDE
CANVAS	FIT	PUMP	TENNIS
CASUAL	FLAT	RUBBER	TOE
CLEAT	FOOT	SANDAL	TREAD
CLOG	GROUND	SHINE	VELCRO
COBBLER	HEEL	SIZE	WOOD
COVER	LACE	SOCK	WORK

Solution on page 258

52

Football Helmet

```
M A S K X C R E Y A L P F P
N V I S O R P E N A L T Y A
B W N L F A C E L B A R U D
A Y O D E F E N S E B O N S
R R I D R A H V Y Q T P I A
S U T S H O G O L U O S F C
T J C O N C U S S I O N O I
R N E F C P U N F P F L R T
A I T F J R N O D M L L M S
P F O E H G A Y T E F A S A
H I R N I M J S G N E G R L
E E P S T U R E H T A E L P
A L E E C I V E D R A U G S
D D T A C K L E M A G E A R
```

BARS	FACE	INJURY	PROTECTION
COLLEGE	FIELD	LEATHER	ROUND
COLORS	FOAM	LOGO	SAFETY
CONCUSSION	FOOTBALL	MASK	SPORT
CRASH	GAME	NFL	STRAP
DEFENSE	GEAR	OFFENSE	TACKLE
DESIGN	GUARD	PADS	TEAM
DEVICE	HARD	PENALTY	TOUCHDOWN
DURABLE	HEAD	PLASTIC	UNIFORM
EQUIPMENT	HIT	PLAYER	VISOR

Solution on page 258

Uniforms

```
X O S K T W S H D Y V A N V
L P K R E U W R K R O T U A
Y P I A I G W X R G Y M R A
E H R T U O C S O D R E S S
S M T U C W D L W O P G E L
R A Z P A N T S O U N D H A
E E D D R A U G O T H A T M
J T N J A E E R T F H B E R
O A S N S L G G T I U L K O
B O O T E C I R A T B O C F
P C E O O A O K T M J U A K
P C D L H P T O E R I S J O
K A O I S I N D R I V E R T
Y R C P E X D J B E F S Q C
```

ALIKE	CODE	JACKET	SCOUT
ARMY	COLOR	JERSEY	SHIRT
BADGE	DRESS	JOB	SHOES
BAND	DRIVER	LOGO	SKIRT
BLOUSE	EMBLEM	NAVY	SPORT
BUTTON	FORMAL	NEAT	SUIT
CAP	GROUP	NURSE	TEAM
CLEAN	GUARD	OUTFIT	TIE
CLOTH	HAT	PANTS	WEAR
COAT	IMAGE	PILOT	WORK

Solution on page 258

Bracelets

```
Z G Y B U R F A M L G O L D
R I H D A E B M R E V L I S
T F G M P N P R E H T A E L
E T S I R W D L N R M A M B
N W V O E A I N A O O E L Y
N R D T S D F R N S D L G N
I A T M E A E D E I T R O B
S P E S N L N R C C E I O C
T G I C T U E A K L H X C U
O G Y R O P L C L S O A C F
N X O R P X K A A E T T I F
E P W O M A N F C R W Y H N
S H C H C T A W E K B E L C
R K B Z S J D S L I N K J E
```

ADORN	COLOR	JEWEL	SILVER
ALLERGY	COPPER	LEATHER	SPORT
ANKLE	CUFF	LINK	STONES
ARM	DESIGN	MEDICAL	STYLE
BAND	DIAMOND	METAL	TENNIS
BEAD	FANCY	NECKLACE	WATCH
BOX	FASHION	PLASTIC	WIRE
BRACELET	GEMS	PRESENT	WOMAN
CHAIN	GIFT	ROUND	WRAP
CLOTH	GOLD	RUBY	WRIST

Solution on page 258

CHAPTER 3: PERSONAL ITEMS   55

Wearing Perfume

```
N S F U Y A S R E W O L F M
O E C N A R F T C V E S S Y
S L A C I M E H C V S C E T
E T R U J N A M I A O E T I
R T O S D N B S U Z R N O U
U O M Y E E N O U F A T N R
T B A L D E C N U R R S X F
X L T M P O O O G Q T E I E
I A H X B I B A L S U I P M
M R E P H E R O M O N E C I
U O R S O F R E L I G H T N
S L A Y D P L E A S A N T I
K F P O O L F A C T I V E N
S N Y A R P S I N C E N S E
```

AMBER	FASHION	NOSE
AROMATHERAPY	FEMININE	NOTES
BODY	FLORAL	ODOR
BOTTLES	FLOWERS	OLFACTIVE
BOUQUET	FRAGRANT	PERFUMERY
CHANEL	FRANCE	PHEROMONE
CHEMICALS	FRUITY	PLEASANT
CITRUS	INCENSE	ROSE
EAU DE COLOGNE	LIGHT	SCENTS
EXPENSIVE	MIXTURES	SMELL
EXTRACTS	MUSKS	SPRAY

Solution on page 259

CHAPTER 4

IT'S DELICIOUS

Cotton Candy

```
R C Q U Y U D C O L O R E D
S R C N U F A A N B S M N V
Y E R A L R I E D O O F P T
C S K O N T R Y F F U L F E
L F S I D D H T S U G A R E
L S V E L N Y G T Q C V N W
S A M I M D E L I C I O U S
L T H C T L A V P L P R P U
W C R A M U S E M E N T S M
N O S E P N C I R C U S I M
E N B D A P E N I H C A M E
B E K C I T S T A S T Y U R
P H K N G K T S S M E L T G
T Z K Y E E E C G A B P M J
```

AIR	FLAVOR	SNACK
AMUSEMENT	FLOSS	SOFT
BAG	FLUFFY	SPUN
BLUE	FOOD	STICK
CANDY	FUN	SUGAR
CARNIVAL	KIDS	SUMMER
CHILDREN	LIGHT	SWEET
CIRCUS	MACHINE	TASTY
COLORED	MELT	THREADLIKE
CONE	MESSY	TREAT
DELICIOUS	PINK	VENDOR

Solution on page 259

Sweet Maple Syrup

```
N T S A F K A E R B R O W N
L I Q U I D M Q U E B E C T
D A R K G N I R P S L H R A
K C I H T A M B U C K E T S
R S M A P L E T R E E S G T
E E K R B G J L O S N O W E
T L N V O N T T A P P I N G
T F A E T E N P N R P O A T
U F I S T W U G G O U I U M
B A D T L E A C R V M T N R
O W A T E N E R O A F R A G
I G N I K A B W M L D O E N
L P A N C A K E S F O E O V
S U C R O S E P I C E R S D
```

AUNT JEMIMA	COLOR	NATURAL	SWEETENER
BAKING	DARK	NEW ENGLAND	TAPPING
BOIL	FLAVOR	PANCAKES	TASTE
BOTTLE	FOOD	POUR	THICK
BREAKFAST	GRADES	QUEBEC	TOPPING
BROWN	HARVEST	RECIPE	TREE SAP
BUCKETS	LIQUID	SNOW	VERMONT
BUTTER	MAINE	SPRING	WAFFLES
CANADIAN	MAPLE TREES	SUCROSE	WARM

Solution on page 259

French Food

```
D O O F O P R O V E N C E Q
T S U R C T R O H S G H P U
O M T E A F O I E G R A S N
R U S N A I L S Y N R M Y S
T S E G A E L D D I M P O E
S H E R B S N K S K A A E L
I R O U X U S T T O E G X B
B O U R G E O I S O R N P A
E O J R F C S R O C C E E T
S M U A R L A V A R E N N E
E B C A L A M A R I C H S G
E S C A R G O T D U C K I E
H Y O P N O E L O P A N V V
C O F F E E P A S T R I E S
```

ARISTOCRACY
BISTRO
BOURGEOIS
BURGUNDY
CAFE
CALAMARI
CHAMPAGNE
CHEESE
COFFEE
COOKING
CREAM

CROISSANTS
DUCK
ESCARGOT
EXPENSIVE
FOIE GRAS
FOOD
HERBS
LA VARENNE
MIDDLE AGES
MUSHROOM
NAPOLEON

PARIS
PASTRIES
PROVENCE
RICH
ROUX
SHORTCRUST
SNAILS
TEA
VEGETABLES

Solution on page 259

Hershey's Kisses

```
Y K I S S Y E H S R E H T S
G A B T C H E R R Y L B S P
K E D B R A N D O O S M K O
R W T I T L E M V P A P E R
A D Y I L L I E A L M O N D
M E D C H O C O L A T E E B
E P N U R W H T F C S L S Y
D P A I Z E R U T A I N I M
A A C P T E T G G C R T L A
R R K C A N S S I S H C V E
T W S T U N E O A F C O E R
G M U N I M U L A E T C R C
N E P A H S Y N A P M O C R
T L K A L L I N A V D A R K
```

ALMOND	CREAMY	HOLIDAY	SMALL
ALUMINUM	DARK	HUGS	SNACK
BAG	DELICIOUS	KISS	TRADEMARK
BRAND	DROPS	LOVE	TREAT
CANDY	EASTER	MELT	VALENTINE
CHERRY	FLAVORS	MINIATURE	VANILLA
CHOCOLATE	FOIL	NUTS	WHITE
CHRISTMAS	GIFT	PAPER	WRAPPED
COCOA	HALLOWEEN	SHAPE	
COMPANY	HERSHEY	SILVER	

Solution on page 260

Yummy Things

```
E K A C A N D Y S O D A Y S
L E F O N D U E B M A P E N
O F R O S T I N G U E I N O
C H N K E A S R S F R E O C
Y H R I I C N E U F B G H A
O G O E N O S G G I I E E B
G R C C W S U D A N E S F R
U A P O O A N U R S A E H P
R P O F R L D F E J A R H U
T E P F B C A R A M E L O D
A S H E R B E T R E S S E D
S W E E T S S C E R E A L I
T P A S T A S P I H C C G N
Y M K A E T S U S H I G P G
```

BACON	CHOCOLATE	GRAPES	SODA
BREAD	COFFEE	HONEY	STEAK
BROWNIES	COOKIE	LASAGNA	SUGAR
BURGER	CREAM	MUFFINS	SUNDAES
CAKE	DESSERT	ORANGES	SUSHI
CANDY	FISH	PASTA	SWEETS
CARAMEL	FONDUE	PIE	TACOS
CEREAL	FRIES	POPCORN	TASTY
CHEESE	FROSTING	PUDDING	YOGURT
CHIPS	FUDGE	SHERBET	

Solution on page 260

62

Hot Chocolate

```
F O X B R D U N K V K O X T
U D Q K F M H P U C F I R E
S Y M Y B S R Z K F I E D K
W U U R O T I A T R A H S S
E M G W Z O C P W T A S T Y
E M B A B V H G G C I D Z G
T Y P T R E T N I W T O H B
K N E E O C O I S C C A N K
H X O R W I R P O T O M N M
M A Y A N P F M V C I I S I
A N O O P S F A O X R R T H
O F L A V O R C Y D G E E E
F U Y Q R E D W O P M A A C
F G J T E K C A P V T W M M
```

BROWN	FIRE	MUG	SUGAR
CAMPING	FLAVOR	PACKET	SWEET
COCOA	FOAM	POWDER	SWISS
COMFORT	FROTH	RICH	TASTY
COZY	FUN	SIP	THICK
CREAM	HEAT	SPICE	TREAT
CUP	HOT	SPOON	WARM
DARK	KIDS	STEAM	WATER
DRINK	MAYAN	STIR	WINTER
DUNK	MIX	STOVE	YUMMY

Solution on page 260

Cheesecake, Please

```
Y F R U I T S N H P S S Z Y
U A L R C R E T I H W H H M
M A H A R G O G U S E C M M
A R K G V O R U G N E I P U
E E A U M O R E N B T R L Y
R C U S T A R D E D J F V E
C I O C H E E S E C I A O E
W P Y O H E L N H L E R B S
J E Q I K E S C L H T E F Y
D C M A M I R I L Y R I A D
P I B O T U N R I R F D N L
X L N Y S G M G Y O I M C O
I S A T H I C K O B R W Y C
V H P K Y I B D Q X M O S Y
```

BAKE	DAIRY	GREECE	SERVE
BERRY	DENSITY	HEAVY	SLICE
CAKE	EGG	LEMON	SMOOTH
CHEESE	FANCY	MIX	SOFT
CHERRY	FILLING	NUTS	SUGAR
COLD	FIRM	PAN	SWEET
COOKING	FLAVOR	PIE	SWIRL
CREAM	FOOD	RECIPE	THICK
CRUST	FRUIT	RICH	WHITE
CUSTARD	GRAHAM	ROUND	YUMMY

Solution on page 260

Fruitcakes

```
S E T A D J C R U M B S K O
Y E N O H J O K E S A T R G
T T C S E I R R E B K U A I
T H G I L A U N N A E N D F
F E N A P I Z R A M D L L T
R A S E P S S R A E K A C S
U V T N A C E C U L N W N N
I Y I D E L I C I O U S E A
T D R H N D R N S T L P V C
S N I S I A R A N N R F O E
G A P L P S E S S A L O M P
G R S O T S H Y U M M Y N F
E B R E C Y C L E D L O A F
S H I P P E D E T N A W N U
```

ANNUAL	DATES	LIGHT	SEASONAL
BAKED	DELICIOUS	LOAF	SHIPPED
BERRIES	DENSE	MARZIPAN	SPICES
BRANDY	EGGS	MOLASSES	SPIRITS
CAKE	FLOUR	OVEN	UNWANTED
CHERRIES	FRUITS	PECANS	WALNUTS
CINNAMON	GIFTS	PINEAPPLE	YUMMY
CITRON	HEAVY	POPULAR	
CRUMBS	HONEY	RAISINS	
DARK	JOKES	RECYCLED	

Solution on page 261

Berry Good

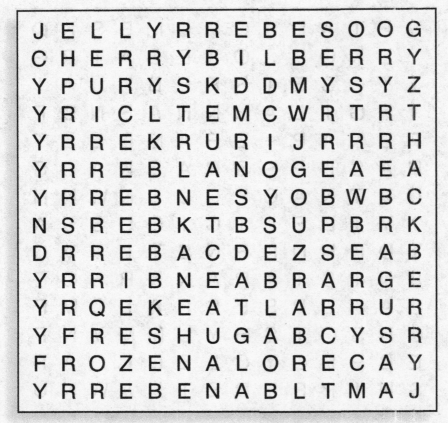

```
J E L L Y R R E B E S O O G
C H E R R Y B I L B E R R Y
Y P U R Y S K D D M Y S Y Z
Y R I C L T E M C W R T R T
Y R R E K R U R I J R R R H
Y R R E B L A N O G E A E A
Y R R E B N E S Y O B W B C
N S R E B K T B S U P B R K
D R R E B A C D E Z S E A B
Y R R I B N E A B R A R G E
Y R Q E K E A T L A R R U R
Y F R E S H U G A B C Y S R
F R O Z E N A L O R E C A Y
Y R R E B E N A B L T M A J
```

ACEROLA	FRESH	PIE
BACCA	FROZEN	RASPBERRY
BANEBERRY	GOOSEBERRY	SEEDS
BILBERRY	HACKBERRY	STRAWBERRY
BLACKBERRY	HUCKLEBERRY	SUGARBERRY
BLUEBERRY	JAM	SYRUP
BOYSENBERRY	JELLY	TART
CHERRY	JOSTABERRY	TEABERRY
CRANBERRY	LOGANBERRY	WINE
ELDERBERRY	MULBERRY	

Solution on page 261

Pizza Toppings

```
S T E A K A N K K K M I P H
K A P N E K C I H C L A M S
B W U I C G O T A M O T A A
O J A C N R G B A S I L R U
N M M T E E M P D I L L T Q
I V E G E T A B L E S H I S
O N A A V R H P R A C D C P
N N T R I V C A P A N N H I
O R B L L P Z R N L F T O C
C O A I O Z K I E C E E K E
A C L C O V P A X S H Z E S
B D L M E S E E H C S O S B
M U S H R O O M S T U N V V
L H B P E P P E R T U N A Y
```

ANCHOVY	GARLIC	SAUCE
ARTICHOKES	HAM	SPICES
BACON	MEATBALLS	SPINACH
BASIL	MOZZARELLA	SQUASH
BEEF	MUSHROOM	STEAK
CHEESE	NUTS	TOMATO
CHICKEN	OLIVE	TUNA
CLAMS	ONION	VEGETABLES
CORN	OREGANO	WATERCRESS
DILL	PEPPER	
EGGPLANT	PINEAPPLE	

Solution on page 261

Fondue

```
K T L E M R A W K E N S B Q
R I S W I N E A S H A R E I
O T E M P E R A T U R E U C
F D I U Q I L H C O O K O B
N U R E Z I T E P P A R U Q
Y T R A P O N A H C N E R F
E C E F R U I T S S I W S S
N O B B F O U N T A I N D V
I M W R E S T A U R A N T K
P M A L T I R I P S E X O I
L U R R E C I P E I D I P R
A N T T H O T S R E W E K S
V A S E D O O F L A M E J C
N L Y S T I C K S M O O T H
```

ALPINE	FOOD	MELT	SMOOTH
APPETIZER	FORK	OIL	SPIRIT LAMP
BROTH	FOUNTAIN	PARTY	STICKS
BURN	FRENCH	POT	STRAWBERRIES
COMMUNAL	FRIENDS	RECIPE	SWISS
COOK	FRUIT	RESTAURANT	TEMPERATURE
CORNSTARCH	FUN	SAUCE	WARM
DIP	HOT	SET	WINE
EAT	KIRSCH	SHARE	
FLAME	LIQUID	SKEWERS	

Solution on page 261

Going Bananas

```
N N F R I E D P I L S N B U
I E B S E E D L E S S A X Y
K P E U I P O A M O N K E Y
S I G R N L O N G A O S K T
E R D D G C G T N D T P A H
D Y S O U T H A M E R I C A
I S W E E T P T T F E H S R
B N A T I U Q I H C S C O V
L A K P D W U O E T S A F E
E C U D O R P N A Z E N T S
E K I L F S E E R T D A G T
P N L T I L P S A N A N A B
G E L O D O O F R O V A L F
Y I L I S T E M A R E B I F
```

BANANA CHIPS	EAT	HARVEST	SKIN
BANANA PUDDING	EDIBLE	LONG	SLIP
BANANA SPLIT	FIBER	MONKEY	SNACK
BUNCH	FLAVOR	PEEL	SOFT
CAKE	FOOD	PIE	SOUTH AMERICA
CHIQUITA	FRIED	PLANTATION	STEM
DESSERT	FRUIT	PRODUCE	SWEET
DOLE	GOOD	RIPEN	TREES
DRIED	GREEN	SEEDLESS	YELLOW

Solution on page 262

Bacon

```
M A P L E Z Z G T A S T Y U
J P K N S T R I P S E H T F
H O I C N E M P T C S I S O
K R O V A L F I U Z A N A O
B K V S P B B T S S U V F D
P Y E K R U T A F O S G K E
I R S G G E N A I D A N A C
G O C G L D G H F I G I E I
S K O R W P O R S U E K R L
O C S I I T I M U M A O B S
X I C L L S O Z A B T O T S
Y H A L A K P A Z H I C N A
L R E E E B W Y S A N A E L
D E V D E I R F Y T G B L T
```

BITS	FATBACK	LEAN	SAUSAGE
BLT	FLAVOR	LETTUCE	SLAB
BREAKFAST	FOOD	MAPLE	SLICED
BRINE	FRIED	OIL	SMOKED
BURGER	GREASE	PAN	SODIUM
CANADIAN	GRILLED	PIGS	STRIPS
COOKING	HAM	PIZZA	TASTY
CRISPY	HICKORY	PORK	THIN
EATING	HOT	SALT	TOAST
EGGS	LARD	SANDWICH	TURKEY

Solution on page 262

Sticky Honey

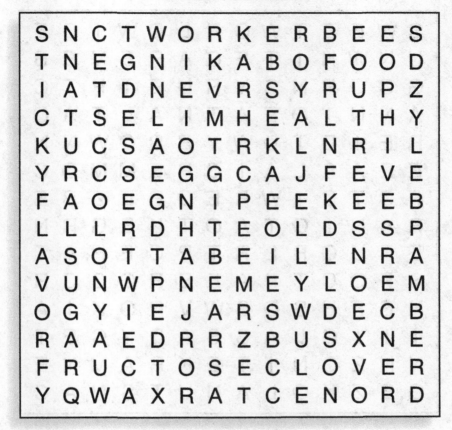

```
S N C T W O R K E R B E E S
T N E G N I K A B O F O O D
I A T D N E V R S Y R U P Z
C T S E L I M H E A L T H Y
K U C S A O T R K L N R I L
Y R C S E G G C A J F E V E
F A O E G N I P E E K E E B
L L L R D H T E O L D S S P
A S O T T A B E I L L N R A
V U N W P N E M E Y L O E M
O G Y I E J A R S W D E C B
R A A E D R R Z B U S X N E
F R U C T O S E C L O V E R
Y Q W A X R A T C E N O R D
```

AMBER	DESSERT	HIVES	STICKY
APIARY	DRONE	JARS	SUGAR
BAKING	ENDEARMENT	MILK	SWEETNESS
BEARS	FLAVOR	NATURAL	SYRUP
BEEKEEPING	FLOWERS	NECTAR	TEA
BREAD	FOOD	POLLEN	THICK
CLOVER	FRUCTOSE	PRODUCT	TREES
COLLECTING	GOLDEN	QUEEN BEE	WAX
COLONY	HEALTHY	ROYAL JELLY	WORKER BEES

Solution on page 262

Coke

```
S W E E T W O R L D W I D E
U N W H I T E G A R E V E B
G C O R N S Y R U P T P T C
A N N I O E A T N A L T A O
R E I D T D W Y B R O W N N
E E A S L A I C R E M M O C
F C T C I W R E O R E Z B E
R A N I O T A O T K E G R N
E F U Q R L R T P C E H A T
S F O C T P A E E R O C C R
H E F H S Q S W V R O K I A
I I I G L A S S A D Y C E T
N N Z G N I T E K R A M N E
G E Z K O L A N U T S N A C
```

ADVERTISING	CORN SYRUP	REFRESHING
ATLANTA	CORPORATION	SODA
BEVERAGE	DIET COKE	SPRITE
BROWN	FIZZ	SUGAR
CAFFEINE	FOUNTAIN	SWEET
CANS	GLASS	WATER
CARBONATED	ICE	WHITE
CHERRY	KOLA NUTS	WORLDWIDE
COLA WARS	MARKETING	ZERO
COMMERCIALS	NEW COKE	
CONCENTRATE	REAL THING	

Solution on page 262

CHAPTER 5

WORDPLAY

Words with an AM

```
Z R Y W G I E S U M A E R C
E M A N N F T O I Y P M A L
R F O A M R L E L P M A S A
O M O V E D A I E R T C N M
A O B A E M M T M F A A K S
M D M Z A A B J A M M E D R
A B A E F M J M F I I F Q M
M M B I M O O A N A N O T A
A M A T E U R G M R G R E X
Z A A M S N C A M S A S A E
I W A E S T A M P W E M M M
N G M M R E M A L A D A L U
G I Z A K D P D R M T H M A
H W T S D D A A F Y C T E A
```

AMATEUR	CAMS	HAM	SAME
AMAZED	CLAM	JAMMED	SAMPLE
AMAZING	CREAM	JAMS	SEAM
AMONG	DAM	LAMB	STAMP
AMOUNT	DREAM	LAME	STREAM
AMUSE	FAME	LAMP	SWAM
BAMBOO	FAMILY	NAME	TAME
BEAM	FAMOUS	NAMING	TAMING
CAME	FOAM	RAM	TEAM
CAMP	GAME	ROAM	WIGWAM

Solution on page 263

74

Words with a SO

```
E S O U P E T F D I L O S G
R Q N S O L V E Q A L S O H
O B R O S B A Z S O F A O B
S O I L I E S S O C I A L N
I O S V G T O W O R R O S N
G B O I X A U K A O S T S S
A H X N P D G L T S E C O O
S T K G N E H H O I I L C R
O U C U N T T M V S A L I R
L O O A M A Z O S R E O E Y
I S S C E L S O D I U M T S
N S O U L O R O L L I O Y O
E T U L O S B A M O O H S R
Y T F O S I O E B E S S X T
```

ABSOLUTE	SOCIAL	SOLID	SORRY
ABSORB	SOCIETY	SOLO	SORT
ALSO	SOCK	SOLUTION	SOUGHT
BLOSSOM	SODIUM	SOLVE	SOUL
GASOLINE	SOFA	SOLVING	SOUND
ISOLATED	SOFT	SOME	SOUP
LASSO	SOIL	SON	SOUR
SCISSORS	SOLAR	SOON	SOUTH
SOAK	SOLD	SORE	SOVIET
SOAP	SOLEMN	SORROW	SOX

Solution on page 263

Words That End with *K*

```
P E A K J O L K M L N K X C
H V R R D D C A K I M X W N
P A C K N U J T C C L E P B
P A A C L H C Q I K C K I H
N O S O F O L K K C O D Y C
U U T L F O R K S U D K K O
W V C J G U W E I E Q C S M
Z T U S B A C L D P D A A U
C U Y M H U Y E V A K R O P
P D X Y B K N A R Z K C E N
C X L S B A C K A E B O I H
A Q I O W A N E R P U O O P
N V V N C O R K D E L O O L
X E A Q C O O K I N K R N K
```

ASK	DARK	HOOK	MARK
BACK	DECK	INK	MILK
BANK	DESK	JUNK	NECK
BARK	DISK	KICK	OAK
BEAK	DOCK	LACK	PACK
BOOK	DUCK	LEAK	PARK
BULK	DUSK	LICK	PEAK
BUNK	FOLK	LOCK	PICK
COOK	FORK	LOOK	PORK
CORK	HAWK	LUCK	RACK

Solution on page 263

Words That Begin with *U*

```
R U M R O F I N U N L E S S
E D N I K N U N T Y I N G J
P Z R I R P C Y W K L V E E
P H S L O O H P S O D G S D
U L S N V N D P U A N Q U I
N L E E R A W A N U E K X S
T O R E O O N H I G S N N P
I R D L T L E N C L Y I U U
E N N N T E V U O I H U N E
U U U G L I E R R E N L L G
Q N A B R U N P N S I C I R
I L A U S U U U E T N J K U
N N R E T T U E N U P S E T
U Q Y D I T N U P W A R D P
```

UGLIER	UNEVEN	UNLIKE	UPPER
UGLIEST	UNHAPPY	UNLOAD	UPSET
UGLY	UNICORN	UNROLL	UPSIDE
UNABLE	UNIFORM	UNSEEN	UPWARD
UNAWARE	UNION	UNTIDY	URBAN
UNCLE	UNIQUE	UNTIE	URGE
UNCOVER	UNIT	UNTIL	USE
UNDER	UNKIND	UNTO	USING
UNDRESS	UNKNOWN	UNTYING	USUAL
UNEASY	UNLESS	UPON	UTTER

Solution on page 263

Words That End with *C*

```
F A B R I C I T N A R F H F
A T H L E T I C M C I S U M
R C E D R A M A T I C R A C
T I R S C Z J T T I G G U I
I N O Y I E M H M T N B E T
S C I T S E M O D E I T L O
T I C T S Z C L T C J C E X
I P I C A I C I M O N O C E
C C N I L N C C I M O T A
I I A G C C I M H T Y H R F
S G H A L P G I G A N T I C
A A C R O H I S T O R I C Z
B M E T A L L I C I T E O P
R O M A N T I C I T S A L E
```

ARC	CUBIC	GIGANTIC	PICNIC
ARTISTIC	DOMESTIC	HEROIC	POETIC
ATHLETIC	DRAMATIC	HISTORIC	RHYTHMIC
ATOMIC	ECONOMIC	MAGIC	ROMANTIC
ATTIC	ELASTIC	MAGNETIC	TOPIC
BASIC	ELECTRIC	MAJESTIC	TRAGIC
CATHOLIC	EXOTIC	MECHANIC	ZINC
CLASSIC	FABRIC	METALLIC	
COMIC	FRANTIC	MUSIC	

Solution on page 264

Words That End with *M*

```
I  N  F  P  D  C  V  B  T  R  S  D  U  B
G  J  O  C  M  O  F  M  D  O  I  Q  C  U
C  E  K  L  C  I  O  M  L  A  P  S  S  C
M  O  R  A  L  O  W  O  E  M  A  E  S  Y
Y  M  L  M  R  I  F  R  M  T  E  M  P  H
G  M  U  M  M  R  O  F  E  M  I  K  S  U
Z  L  O  O  A  U  X  U  T  L  B  T  M  M
P  N  T  O  E  O  R  P  S  J  I  M  I  R
L  A  U  L  B  D  F  D  R  W  D  H  E  M
G  C  F  U  Q  Q  V  M  I  A  A  G  O  W
J  Z  B  X  Q  F  M  G  U  M  E  M  M  D
B  R  L  O  O  P  G  Q  Z  M  I  A  U  G
S  J  U  K  C  F  H  M  R  A  R  D  W  S
Q  B  I  E  E  E  F  S  J  C  E  J  Q  G
```

AIM	FILM	HIM	RIM
ARM	FIRM	HUM	ROAM
ATOM	FOAM	ITEM	ROOM
BEAM	FORM	LOOM	SEAM
BOOM	FROM	MOM	SEEM
CALM	GERM	MUM	SKIM
CLAM	GUM	PALM	SLIM
DAM	GYM	PLUM	STEM
DIM	HAM	POEM	SUM
DRUM	HEM	RAM	SWAM

Solution on page 264

Words with a BE

```
Z Y N A E B E C A M E H D Q
C T B P A B C U B E S T D W
E U A R E V A E B E H I N D
B A B A B G M V B E L D E B
O E D E R O F E B E L O B T
R B A T C Y H E B A L O N D
P C W E B A R E B O P I W G
H I B E V R L E M E L N E G
F U E E Y L L T T A A G D F
T J A B N T E R G S Y M I F
K E T E Z C I B B Y A B S A
X T K A E B H Y E B O E E C
Y M F R E E X U G N I E B V
P I V I M T Z W V O T Z R K
```

BARBER	BEAVER	BELIEF	BEST
BEACH	BECAME	BELL	BET
BEAD	BECOME	BELONG	CUBE
BEAK	BED	BELOW	GLOBE
BEAM	BEE	BELT	LABEL
BEAN	BEFORE	BENCH	MAYBE
BEAR	BEG	BEND	OBEY
BEAST	BEHAVE	BENT	ROBE
BEAT	BEHIND	BERRY	TRIBE
BEAUTY	BEING	BESIDE	TUBE

Solution on page 264

Rhymes with Belle

```
D G C S M E L L Z I L L E Y
F E L L N R W F X M L C A C
Q U E L L E P O R P E A O W
M O T E L S L R N E S R S M
X C O M P E L E D L N T H A
M L H L P L W T I E A E E T
O E L S L L L E L N L L L T
R G I E E E I L R Q A L L E
E D C T X Z S L E A K D C L
L L S H J A A O E N F A E E
A A L E A G M E C V R M U U
P N L E T N O M Y M R A R G
E L L E W S E P E O C A D I
L E P E R D U L H G Q W C M
```

ANSEL	DARNELL	HOTEL	PASTEL
CARMEL	DELL	IMPEL	PROPEL
CARTEL	DISPEL	JELL	QUELL
CARVEL	DWELL	LAPEL	REPEL
CELL	FAREWELL	MATTEL	RESELL
CHANEL	FELL	MAXELL	SHELL
COMPEL	FORETELL	MIGUEL	SMELL
CORNELL	GAZELLE	MONTEL	SWELL
COSELL	GEL	MOREL	YELL
DANIELE	HORMEL	MOTEL	

Solution on page 264

Words on PAR

```
D E T R A P E D A R A P M T
E K A P P A R E N T L Y N R
S N O S I R A P M O C V C A
U A P P R E P A R A T I O N
T P A R T N E R S H I P M S
A A R E P T D T E S G A P P
R R A P A H E M T K N R A A
A T L A R E K E U R I C R R
P M L R T S R N H A K E I E
P E E E L E A T C P R L N N
A N L D Y S P S A S A S G T
R T S P A R A G R A P H S I
T B V S E P A R A T I N G N
S Q E R U T R A P E D O C G
```

APARTMENT	PARADE	PARTNERSHIP
APPARATUS	PARAGRAPHS	PARTS
APPARENTLY	PARALLELS	PREPARATION
COMPARING	PARCELS	PREPARED
COMPARISONS	PARENTHESES	SEPARATING
DEPARTED	PARENTING	SPARKS
DEPARTMENTS	PARKED	TRANSPARENT
DEPARTURE	PARKING	
PARACHUTES	PARTLY	

Solution on page 265

Words with *Es*

```
F R E E Z E V E E L S N O W
Y Z D E S E R V E N E E S S
E Z E E R B E L I E V E E E
B D E G R E M E W V R D A V
R P E E R E D T I E E L W E
E K D E E P E S T L S E E R
V R F X E B T H E E E X E E
E E R T B N C M C Z R P D P
R L E R E D E N T E R E D E
S E P E E N L M C S T N T E
E A E M T Q E E I E A S Z K
C S E E L T I D E E P E R X
R E L I E V E R D H S R A D
S E S E E G G S J C D F H V
```

BEETLE	ELECTED	GEESE	RESERVE
BELIEVE	ELEMENT	GREETED	REVERSE
BETWEEN	ELEVEN	KEEPER	SEAWEED
BREEZE	EMERGED	NEEDLE	SEEMED
CHEERED	ENEMIES	PEERED	SETTEE
CHEESE	ENTERED	RECEIVE	SEVERE
DEEPER	EXPENSE	REFEREE	SLEEPER
DEEPEST	EXTREME	RELEASE	SLEEVE
DESERVE	FREEZE	RELIEVE	

Solution on page 265

Words with an EAR

```
M Y L R A E N U C L E A R O
P E A R L S F Y T R A E H Q
X T E A R I N G N I R A E B
S W E A R L I E R A E A A S
G N E A R E S T E A R S R H
N G D E R A E L C N A A I T
I C I R E L C Y I L E E N R
R C L E A R I N G B N R G A
A S B E R E G E H C A R A E
E R L E A S H T S E N R A E
W A F E A R F U L T W T W C
H E A R S R L E A R N E D W
N F E A R E D Y L R A E D I
A X H E A R T S N R A E L A
```

BEARDS	EARLIER	HEARD	NEAREST
BEARING	EARLIEST	HEARING	NEARLY
BEARS	EARNEST	HEARS	NUCLEAR
CLEARED	EARNINGS	HEARTS	PEARLS
CLEARER	EARTHS	HEARTY	REAR
CLEARING	FEARED	LEARNED	SWEAR
CLEARLY	FEARFUL	LEARNS	TEARING
DEARLY	FEARS	LEARNT	TEARS
EARACHE	GEARS	NEARER	WEARING

Solution on page 265

Words That Begin with *F*

```
C Y K E T S A F E E T H W K
U L N R L R A E F I N S E B
O I I P E M J X I E R I F D
F A D E E F A N L N L X V H
F F F C F I S T E Z H L N L
G B A A T O A B D S X R E D
Z F C D L A G G I F D O E B
G E T T E L K F U N T F F K
L R X I F J I T I F A L I A
K N F V P I H F U R F Y W T
Z Q C W N G L Y W Y M F O M
W R I I B J J M L U M L T L
X L H N B Z B F D H W K L Z
H K K X J Z S W E N P V P S
```

FACE	FAT	FIG	FIST
FACT	FEAR	FILE	FIT
FADE	FED	FILL	FIX
FAIL	FEED	FILM	FLY
FAIR	FEEL	FIND	FOG
FALL	FEET	FINE	FOR
FAME	FELL	FINS	FOX
FAN	FELT	FIRE	FRY
FAR	FERN	FIRM	FUN
FAST	FEW	FISH	FUR

Solution on page 265

Words with TOP

```
M B I G T O P T H C D M Z E
P H O T O P L A Y A Y U Z X
O B T O P S Y T U R V Y T J
T E O P O S T S H R A A O J
T S P N G A A U K O E K P S
A A O A R R O P Y T H E S C
L O N M A B C O K T P P I I
F N Y E P P P T Y O O O D P
L I M A H O O C S P T T E O
U P Y L Y T T O P D O G S T
P S N P O T L L O R O A K P
O P S S E L P O T E E R T A
T O P S O I L M U S N W O L
S T I P T O P M A S T Z P S
```

AUTOPSY
BIG TOP
CARROT TOP
DESKTOP
FLATTOP
LAPTOP
OCTOPUS
PHOTOPLAY
RAGTOP
ROLL TOP
STOP

TIPTOP
TOP BRASS
TOP DOGS
TOP DRESS
TOP HEAVY
TOP NAME
TOPCOAT
TOPEKA
TOPICS
TOPLESS
TOPMAST

TOPMOST
TOPOGRAPHY
TOPONYMY
TOPSIDE
TOPSOIL
TOPSPIN
TOPSY TURVY
TREETOP
ZZ TOP

Solution on page 266

Rhymes with Sue

```
V C N T Z L Z L T G C X D D
X B O F L E W B W V T R Y Q
N R H M O E B E O N A C F K
U U W B H T R A L D T B A C
F R E C Y D R I M B T Z F O
C I H S S Y S N H B O F O O
E W W T W V N T N O O H E G
W N E F E J O A E N S O S W
O W D K L V Q O D O C T P V
V E W G S I O U X I R W E D
W I Y R H H E M M E E E W L
F V O E A G U A W R W U W X
F L U W G U L H B E A L L E
J C Q J G H G S N A Q B A C
```

ADIEU	DEW	HUGH	STEW
BAMBOO	DREW	KAZOO	STREW
BLEW	EWE	NEW	TATTOO
BLUE	FEW	SCREW	THRU
BREW	FLEW	SHAMU	TWO
CANOE	FLU	SHOO	VIEW
CHEW	FONDUE	SIOUX	WAHOO
CLUE	GLUE	SKEW	WHEW
COO	GOO	SLEW	WHO
CUE	GREW	SPEW	YOU

Solution on page 266

Words That Begin with *I*

```
X J A X L M A E V O R P M I
I E T E L D I N J U R Y D N
N Q D S I I M I T A T E J F
S D N N I S M G E T A D L A
I I A I I S E A I C I U B N
D N L N N U N M G N I L D T
E S S C E P I T E N C N S
T U I E H A G E M O D N A I
I R I R C N N K R M E I L C
V E T T O T N I D N E T N I
N M S R C I S R O O D N I C
I T E R U J N I N F G Y S L
P N L T N E V N I N C O M E
P B F I I S H N N I O Z Y I
```

ICE	IMMENSE	INJURE	INTEND
ICICLE	IMPACT	INJURY	INTENT
ICY	IMPROVE	INK	INTO
IDEA	INCH	INLAND	INVENT
IDLE	INCLUDE	INN	INVITE
IGNORE	INCOME	INSECT	IRON
ILL	INDEED	INSERT	ISLAND
IMAGE	INDEX	INSIDE	ISSUE
IMAGINE	INDOORS	INSIST	ITEM
IMITATE	INFANT	INSURE	ITSELF

Solution on page 266

CHAPTER 6

PEOPLE

Alexander Graham Bell

N M F B H P A R G O N O H P
A E R O N A U T I C S Y G H
S T C A N A D I A N D G R Y
E A R O S S E F O R P O U S
G L S H K D N U O S I L B I
A D U C P R A F F N O O N C
S E I E L A O I V N N N I I
S T N E M I R E P X E H D S
E E E P L S N G F K E C E T
M C G S T T E E E A R E V K
Y T I C I R T C E L E T I R
A O N O I T U C O L E D C O
T R N A C I R E M A X T E W
T S I T N E I C S U O M A F

AERONAUTICS	FAMOUS	PIONEER
AMERICAN	FIRST	PROFESSOR
ATT	GENIUS	SCIENTIST
CANADIAN	HYDROFOILS	SOUND
DEAF	INVENTIONS	SPEECH
DEVICE	LINE	TECHNOLOGY
EDINBURGH	MESSAGES	TELEGRAPH
ELECTRICITY	METAL DETECTOR	WORK
ELOCUTION	PHONOGRAPH	
EXPERIMENTS	PHYSICIST	

Solution on page 266

Elvis Impersonators

```
N K M O V I E Y D O R A P D
P I I S G N I D D E W T C A
R N C W U G E V E N T S R N
E G R H I N E S T O N E S C
S H O W T G G Y U R N O T E
L H P H A I R L U I U A A M
E I H S R L I B A N T M G U
Y P O C E P E T D S E A E T
D S N W C D R A E M S T S S
E B E U I E L Q P N U E D O
M J R S T I U H A B T U S C
O L I N K I I F I N G R C A
C N E E N S M R O F R E P P
G C I S U M T C V O I C E E
```

ACT	FANS	MUSIC	STAGE
AMATEUR	GUITAR	PARODY	SUIT
CAPE	HAIR	PERFORM	SUNGLASSES
COMEDY	HIPS	PRESLEY	TRIBUTE
CONTEST	JEWELRY	RHINESTONES	VEGAS
COPY	KING	SEQUINS	VOICE
COSTUME	LIP CURL	SHOW	WEDDINGS
DANCE	MEMPHIS	SIDEBURNS	WIG
ENTERTAINER	MICROPHONE	SING	
EVENTS	MOVIE	SOUND ALIKE	

Solution on page 267

Mother Teresa

```
A G N I Y D D E S S E L B V
H N O A D V O C A T E H A I
E I T C H A R I T Y C T L R
L V C A R I N G L O I I B H
P O V E R T Y O M C P A A S
S L Y N H T H P A O E F N A
E U U O Y R A N O I S S I M
L N O G Y S O R P E L H A D
F D I I S M I R A C L E N A
L V T I G P S N A H P R O P
E G O E Z I R P L E B O N V
S N O A C I L E G N A M O W
S I N D I A N E R D L I H C
E P O P L S P I R I T U A L
```

ADVOCATE	DYING	LOVING	POVERTY
ALBANIAN	FAITH	MIRACLE	RELIGIOUS
ANGELIC	GIVE	MISSIONARY	SAINTHOOD
BHARAT RATNA	GOD	NOBEL PRIZE	SELFLESS
BLESSED	HELP	NUN	SPIRITUAL
CARING	HERO	ORPHANS	VATICAN
CHARITY	HOLY	PADMA SHRI	WOMAN
CHILDREN	INDIAN	POOR	
COMPASSION	LEPROSY	POPE	

Solution on page 267

Al Capone

```
E A M B D E T A C I D N Y S
J N A O E M Y P R I S O N U
S A F O A A R R E S T I N Y
R I I T D S O O K O Z T C N
E L A L C S T H R O A A S Y
T A X E V A S I O N R Z U L
S T M G L C I B Y S T I O K
G I O G S R H I W T A N I O
N G N I R E E T E K C A R O
A U E N A F B I N R L G O R
G N Y G G B L O O D A R T B
K S E L I O T N E S S O O B
B O S S C S M U G G L I N G
C R I M I N A L F A M I L Y
```

ALCATRAZ	ELIOT NESS	MONEY
ARREST	FAMILY	NEW YORK
BLOOD	FBI	NOTORIOUS
BOOTLEGGING	GANGSTERS	ORGANIZATION
BOSS	GUNS	PRISON
BROOKLYN	HISTORY	PROHIBITION
CARS	ITALIAN	RACKETEERING
CIGARS	JAIL	SMUGGLING
CRIMINAL	MAFIA	SYNDICATE
DEAD	MASSACRE	TAX EVASION

Solution on page 267

Audrey Hepburn

```
A M E C A F Y N N U F N L E
B T N A I R A T I N A M U H
R I I G O L D E N G L O B E
E F H M N A I G L E B I E C
A F T Y D M L O D T T N A L
K A N F I E O C S T O C U A
F N A A N N H V O C T H T S
A Y G I E I N D I B A A I S
S S E R T C A T S E B R F I
T D L L S E M M Y M S A U C
Y R E A R M O T H E R D L I
L A B D R E R R E F L E M G
E W N Y D O O W Y L L O H I
B A L L E R I N A C T I N G
```

ACTING	CLASSIC	MOTHER
ANDREA DOTTI	ELEGANT	MOVIES
AWARDS	EMMY	MY FAIR LADY
BALLERINA	FUNNY FACE	ONDINE
BEAUTIFUL	GIGI	OSCAR
BELGIAN	GOLDEN GLOBE	ROMAN HOLIDAY
BEST ACTRESS	HOLLYWOOD	STYLE
BREAKFAST	HUMANITARIAN	THIN
CHARADE	ICON	TIFFANYS
CINEMA	MEL FERRER	

Solution on page 267

Johnny Appleseed

```
S P F A R M E R T S H E D M
N W E K S G E O D G T R Q I
U O E N O E O E N O E O H S
R N F D N F E I O H B L T S
S F B O E S T R I I A K L I
E N I R E N Y K T O Z L A O
R P A L A V B L A E I O E N
Y B P L M B O O V M L F H A
M P P W E S T L R A E P D R
A N I M A L S E E G N N P Y
N T I U R F D P S T I I O A
N E R D L I H C N K O A A H
L E G A C Y S K O O B P N M
F J N A M P A H C N H O J Q
```

ANIMALS	FARMER	MISSIONARY
APPLE SEEDS	FILMS	NURSERYMAN
APPLE TREES	FOLKLORE	OHIO
BAREFOOT	FRUIT	PENNSYLVANIA
BOOKS	HEALTH	PIONEER
CHILDREN	JOHN CHAPMAN	PLANTING
CIDER MILLS	KIND	POT
CONSERVATION	LEGACY	SWEDENBORGIAN
ELIZABETH	LOVE	WEST

Solution on page 268

Hulk Hogan

```
T R X Y T I R B E L E C X S
E D E Q H U L K R U L E S E R
R N H A B I C E P S B J U H
R O E H L T B S R R M S O C
Y L A O N I C K O O U M M T
C B V L F T T O F C R A A A
H O Y L S L K Y E K L C F M
A D W Y J E O R S Y A K T U
M Y E W H B I R S H Y D O S
P S I O F N O V I D O O O C
I L G O G T X Q O D R W B U
O A H D C N D L N M A N G L
N M T A H U L K A M A N I A
L N O I S I V E L E T K B R
```

ACTOR	FAMOUS	PROFESSIONAL
BELT	FLORIDA	REALITY SHOW
BICEPS	HEAVYWEIGHT	RING
BIG BOOT	HOLLYWOOD	ROCKY
BLOND	HULK RULES	ROYAL RUMBLE
BODY SLAM	HULKAMANIA	SMACKDOWN
BROOKE HOGAN	MATCHES	TELEVISION
CELEBRITY	MOVIES	TERRY
CHAMPION	MUSCULAR	TITLE
DOLL	NICK	WWF

Solution on page 268

John Glenn

```
A E A R T H L S H U T T L E
U S K Y A T R A I N I N G N
N H T O R B I T S E N A T E
I V I R C Y R A T I L I M W
F H O N O R S C O M B A T S
O E I R M N L Y R U C R E M
R O C K E T A D I D N A C A
M O F R D H D U C A S A N W
H H T F O O E S T A R S I A
C N Y A L F M I S S I O N R
N O A L I Y R E V O C S I D
U O C M J V I I N A V Y M S
A M E R I C A N A R E T E V
L T S R I F L I G H T J G B
```

AIR FORCE	EARTH	MERCURY	SENATE
AIR MEDAL	FIRST	MILITARY	SHUTTLE
AMERICA	FLIGHT	MISSION	SKY
ASTRONAUT	FLYING	MOON	STARS
AVIATOR	GEMINI	NASA	TRAINING
AWARDS	HERO	NAVY	UNIFORM
CANDIDATE	HISTORIC	NEWS	VETERAN
COMBAT	HONORS	OHIO	
DEMOCRAT	LAUNCH	ORBIT	
DISCOVERY	MAN	ROCKET	

Solution on page 268

Helen Keller

```
E Y L D E N G I A P M A C O
G E I I N L A C I T I L O P
A G A S A Y S R E T A W M A
U A R A C R I C T L D H M U
G R B B I O G R A P H Y U T
N U M I R T N B C B O L N H
A O S L E S A J O Z A E I O
L C I I M M D O V R C C C R
E V L T A E K U D Y T T A P
F I A Y A W O M A N I U T D
T S I F I C A P O G V R E N
I I C D W S U M O V I E F I
S O O V T N E D U T S R V L
T N S G N I R A E H T R L B
```

ACTIVIST	COURAGE	PATTY DUKE
ADVOCATE	DEAF	POLITICAL
ALABAMA	DISABILITY	SIGN
AMERICAN	EDUCATION	SOCIALISM
AUTHOR	GIRL	STORY
BIOGRAPHY	HEARING	STUDENT
BLIND	LANGUAGE	VISION
BOOK	LECTURER	WATER
BRAIL	LEFTIST	WOMAN
CAMPAIGNED	MOVIE	
COMMUNICATE	PACIFIST	

Solution on page 268

Oprah

```
C L N O I S I V E L E T A S
O U U S S E R T C A N N P S
L F J G U T I B A E I B E O
O S S L O K C I M M Z G R L
R S W I R M H L A M A A S T
P E E H E T A L B Y G Y O H
U C I P N E R I O Z A L N G
R C V R E I P O D S M E A I
P U R D G D O N E E O K L E
L S E H Y K C A L B M I I W
E N T E R T A I N M E N T O
X S N P O W E R F U L G Y M
C O I N F L U E N T I A L E
M I S S I S S I P P I C O N
```

ACTRESS
ANIMAL RIGHTS
BILLIONAIRE
BLACK
COLOR PURPLE
DIET
DR PHIL
EMMY
ENTERTAINMENT

GAYLE KING
GENEROUS
HARPO
ICON
INFLUENTIAL
INTERVIEWS
MEDIA MOGUL
MISSISSIPPI
MONEY

O MAGAZINE
OBAMA
PERSONALITY
POWERFUL
RICH
SUCCESSFUL
TELEVISION
WEIGHT LOSS
WOMEN

Solution on page 269

James Dean

```
S P O R T S C A R Q X H N Q
A M N A I N R O F I L A C U
L Y V E I F T S N O T I Y A
M S T X D C C D P A N R M K
I T J I A E I I L Y E E O E
N E E M R A F I N T D O T R
E R L L N B E O E O I E O A
O I C A E W E M T X C T R T
F O N H O V E L Y S C I C S
G U C O O C I X E A A D Y E
I S D S K L E S T C R E C I
A W A R D S A S I O A A L V
N L A I C R E M M O C T E O
T P Z L E B E R E L N H C M
```

AWARDS	EAST OF EDEN	NATALIE WOOD
BEST ACTOR	FILM ACTOR	PARK CEMETERY
CALIFORNIA	GIANT	QUAKER
CAR ACCIDENT	HAIR	REBEL
CELEBRITY	ICONIC	SAL MINEO
CHOLAME	INDIANA	SEXY
COMMERCIAL	MOTORCYCLE	SPORTS CAR
COOL	MOVIE STAR	SPYDER
DEATH	MYSTERIOUS	TELEVISION

Solution on page 269

Woody Guthrie

```
T D W O O D R O W R I T E R R
R E G E E S E T E P A M W E
E P F A M I L Y A C Q U E C
C R N C U A R T I S T B S A
N E E I S F F N N T L L T E
O S R R I I O F R W I A E P
C S D E C M L O O N B M R R
O I L M R E U B F L A O N O
U O I A G B T L I G L H M T
N N H A A S U U L U L A O E
T W C D U E P E A I A L H S
R Y O D N A L S C T D K U T
Y U E C N E I D U A S O N G
R P E R F O R M E R A D I O
```

ALBUM
AMERICA
ARTIST
AUDIENCE
BALLAD
BLUES
CALIFORNIA
CHILDREN
CONCERT
COUNTRY
DEPRESSION

DUST BOWL
FAMILY
GUITAR
HALL OF FAME
HARMONICA
INFLUENCE
LAND
LEGACY
MUSIC
OKLAHOMA
OLD

PEACE
PERFORMER
PETE SEEGER
PROTEST
RADIO
SONG
TROUBADOUR
WESTERN
WOODROW
WRITER

Solution on page 269

Johnny Cash

```
E C H I G H W A Y M E N W L
L I A J J U N E C A R T E R
A S V R E L O H O C L A R E
K U C O T T S I T R A E E T
A M I I M E I S G U R D M I
D Y C C S O R G U I T A R R
D R L H O U P F F B N C O W
I T A B R N M F A I L H F G
C N S A Z I O L N M T U R N
T U S N C G S B E U I G E O
I O I D N T L T A P T L P S
O C C I A A O V I E S R Y E
N G R R C Z F R F A M O U S
R O C K A B I L L Y N S G H
```

ACTOR	COUNTRY MUSIC	JUNE CARTER
ADDICTION	DRUGS	MAN IN BLACK
ALCOHOL	FAMOUS	MOVIE
ARTIST	FOLSOM PRISON	PERFORMER
AUTHOR	GOSPEL MUSIC	RING OF FIRE
BAND	GUITAR	ROCKABILLY
BLUES	HIGHWAYMEN	SONGWRITER
CARTER FAMILY	HURT	STAR
CHRISTIAN	ICON	SUE
CLASSIC	JAIL	

Solution on page 269

Captain Kangaroo

```
B C S G C L A U G H T E R F
O H I G N I N R O M G E T U
B I L L C O S B Y R T R N N
N L L A M L S S E C E W A O
O D Y N O K H E A A O M C I
O R L O O O N R S L A S A S
T E G I S J A U C N C T P I
R N N T E H R T A K Y N T V
A S I A C E C N E I D U A E
C T N C O B A E M E H T I L
I S R U I B S V K I D S N E
S E A D D H Q D P U P P E T
U U E E A Y L A M B C H O P
M G L N R Y M A R G O R P D
```

ADVENTURES
AUDIENCE
BANANA MAN
BILL COSBY
BOB
CAPTAIN
CARTOON
CBS
CHARACTER

CHILDREN
CLASSIC
CLOWN
EDUCATIONAL
FUN
GREEN JEANS
GUESTS
HOST
KEESHAN

KIDS
LAMB CHOP
LAUGHTER
LEARNING
MOOSE
MORNING
MUSIC
PROGRAM
PUPPET

RADIO
SILLY
SONG
STUNTS
TELEVISION
THEME
TREASURE

Solution on page 270

Jerry Seinfeld

```
A P R S U N C L E L E O N S
U O A H E K S T A N D U P E
T R L O N R E R I T A S M I
H S U W B O R I C H P G O N
O C P E C Y I H E Q A B N F
R H O F D W H S P M R R O E
E E P A E E S Y I O T O L L
C V V C I N I F S V M O O D
U I R S R I W F O I E K G R
D T O K R A E U D E N L U E
O A T N A L J P E S T Y E H
R E C O M E D I A N W N C T
P R A M A N H A T T A N D A
A C I S S E J S U O M A F F
```

ACTOR	JEWISH	PORSCHE
APARTMENT	LARRY DAVID	PRODUCER
AUTHOR	MANHATTAN	PUFFY SHIRT
BROOKLYN	MARRIED	RICH
COMEDIAN	MONKS CAFE	SATIRE
CREATIVE	MONOLOGUE	SEINFELD
ELAINE	MOVIES	SHOW
EPISODE	NBC	STAND UP
FAMOUS	NEW YORK	TELEVISION
FATHER	NYC	UNCLE LEO
JESSICA	POPULAR	

Solution on page 270

CHAPTER 7

ALL NATURAL

Insect Life

```
K L I S T A N G N I Y L F S
Y S T I N G E R U T A N Y P
L B E W O S A C D M I G W S
L L S E S T D R I O O U B A
A W E D I S R N A L O U R W
M A T E O E A S O C T F X F
S R I P P P G M W T H A O S
P C M I E U O I E S R N T R
E R R T B T N R E O E T I E
C I E N N G F I H M G E U D
I C T E S L L T O T G N Q I
E K Y C Y F Y D O B R N S P
S E L T E E B I T E S A O S
S T F L E A V R A L W E M D
```

ABDOMEN	CENTIPEDE	FOOD	SMALL
ANIMAL	CRAWL	FRUIT	SPECIES
ANTENNAE	CRICKET	GNATS	SPIDERS
ARACHNID	DRAGONFLY	LARVAE	STING
ARTHROPODS	EGG	LICE	TERMITES
BEETLES	ENTOMOLOGY	MOSQUITO	THORAX
BITES	EYES	NATURE	WASPS
BODY	FLEA	PESTS	WEB
BUGS	FLIES	POISON	WINGS
BUTTERFLY	FLYING	SILK	

Solution on page 270

Penguins Are Birds

```
O D E X U T X A N I M A L R
E I V O M L E L D D A W E H
G B L A C K R I L L C T O N
G W T A I N O G A T A P R E
S E I C E P S N O W R N A W
S O U T H E R N R D O G L Z
F L I G H T L E S S N Z O E
S G K A E B D R D I I C P A
G N W T I N E I M A E C I L
N I I R U H V M I A T Z H A
I H D G T I I Y N O L O C N
W S N A N W E M P E R O R D
E I E G S D N A L S I C A M
K F L I P P E R S E A T M C
```

ANIMAL	FLIGHTLESS	MOVIE	SWIMMING
BEAK	FLIPPERS	NEW ZEALAND	TUXEDO
BIRDS	HOP	OCEAN	UNDERWATER
BLACK	ICE	PATAGONIA	WADDLE
COLONY	ISLANDS	POLAR	WHITE
DIVING	KING	PREDATOR	WINGS
EGGS	KRILL	SEA	ZOO
EMPEROR	MACARONI	SNOW	
FEATHERS	MARCH	SOUTHERN	
FISHING	MATES	SPECIES	

Solution on page 270

Great White Shark

```
E L R E T A W H A L E K E E E
I E U O S P E C I E S G V Z
D O O F P R E Y H D U W E I
R T O U R I S M Y H O V A S
H D A N G E R O U S I O T J
G T M U H C W I M S C R L H
R L H K S I Q O S O O C S B
E A T C I T V E P N R O K O
T M S A A I R M G I E A I A
N M W T E G A A G F F S N T
U A I T G R E L L I K T K S
H M M A I N R O F I L A C A
T U O N S U L E G R A L K F
T E E T H B I G K R A H S E
```

AGGRESSIVE
ATTACK
AUSTRALIA
BIG
BLOOD
BOAT
CAGE
CALIFORNIA
CHUM
COASTAL

DANGEROUS
EAT
FAST
FEROCIOUS
FIN
FOOD
GILLS
HAWAII
HUGE
HUNTER

JAWS
KILLER
LARGE
MAMMAL
MARINE
MOVIE
POWERFUL
PREY
SHARK
SIZE

SKIN
SNOUT
SPECIES
STRONG
SWIM
TEETH
TOOTH
TOURISM
WATER
WHALE

Solution on page 271

Amazing Trees

```
R L S H R U B R R B S T P E
S D L S O S G I W T E A Y A
S N T A O K N U R T L E P R
E A H S T G N I B M I L C T
R L G P S G N I T N A L P H
P D I E G R O W I N G E M R
Y O L C T F I E D W O E E A
C O N I F E R S A X T L K D
R W U E B U C T Y S P K R E
I R S S T A E G Y P O N A C
F K R A P R E S A I R L B U
A T N E M N O R I V N E D R
L B R A N C H E S T N U T P
L F O R E S T S E V A E L S
```

AIR	CONIFERS	LANDSCAPE	SAP
APPLE	CYPRESS	LEAVES	SHRUB
ASH	EARTH	NATURE	SPECIES
BARK	ECOSYSTEM	OLD	SPRUCE
BEECH	ENVIRONMENT	OXYGEN	SUNLIGHT
BRANCHES	FALL	PALM	TALL
CANOPY	FIR	PARK	TRUNK
CEDAR	FORESTS	PLANTING	TWIGS
CHESTNUT	FRUIT	RINGS	WATER
CLIMBING	GROWING	ROOTS	WOODLAND

Solution on page 271

Cold Blood

```
S I S Y S Q U A M A T A E H
R G E E G E C K O S I O S W
E U K Z T O N A E T I B D W
P A A D O U L I N O G A R D
I N N C R O C O D I L I A L
V A S H D N D S T U M V Z L
L I W A I O L M S E T A I A
T B N M N I I O E C P S L M
A I O E O T G N L N A R E S
I H H L S U H I T H E L E T
L P T E A L T T R V S E E H
S M Y O U O R O U G H R R S
Q A P N R V E R T E B R A G
K N I K S E C N E I C S K M
```

AMPHIBIAN
ANIMALS
BITE
BOA
CHAMELEON
CROCODILIA
DINOSAURS
DRAGON
EVOLUTION

GECKO
GREEN
HEAT
HERPETOLOGY
IGUANA
LAND
LIGHT
LIZARDS
MARSH

MONITOR
PYTHON
ROUGH
SCALES
SCIENCE
SCUTES
SEA
SKINK
SMALL

SNAKES
SPHENODONTIA
SQUAMATA
TAILS
TESTUDINES
TURTLES
VERTEBRA
VIPER
ZOO

Solution on page 271

Dachshunds

```
L S S I Y E T U C R B D J F
Z D T W R G E R M A N N B W
F U R R T S X C C B N E R H
I H A K O O M K J B G I I I
N C I S C H N A H I S R N T
I L N C H A S E L T O F D E
M J O E O T L E U L O C L K
D S T N U H G B O H O O E T
T A A T N S B C B S V N M I
N K P G D Y K B P A N H G S
J S T E P E R E N E I W D K
L W C P A O A T L L A Y O L
A A U A W O B R L A Q Y G A
R P S N O U T D S K R R O W
```

AKC	DOG	LONG	SIT
BACK	EARS	LOYAL	SMALL
BARK	FRIEND	MINI	SMOOTH
BLACK	FUR	PAWS	SNOUT
BRINDLE	GERMAN	PET	STUBBY
BROWN	HOUND	PUPPY	TAN
CANINE	HUNT	RABBIT	TRAIN
CHASE	KENNEL	RACE	WALK
COLOR	LEASH	SCENT	WHITE
CUTE	LEGS	SHORT	WIENER

Solution on page 271

Mules

```
A E R I D E L L U P T E A M
M X L T R A N S P O R T H G
A O Y A R G O C A R T D T N
R K L B M R G L L N E E G I
E S C L L I A T E T P H N R
L T K A Y C W G A N O F E P
U U B C P U I C E O E P R S
M B E K O L I D V R A K T F
W B A U L T R E T T Y V S F
O O S E S U S I I B H M T O
L R T E B R L E R R O S R M
P N M I A E N E V P G E O A
I O S E Y T E I K I C K N N
D K R O W D S A D D L E G E
```

AGRICULTURE	GRAY	MOLLY	SORREL
ARMY	HOOVES	MULE	STRENGTH
BAY	INFERTILE	OFFSPRING	STRONG
BEAST	INTELLIGENT	PACK	STUBBORN
BLACK	KICK	PATIENT	TAIL
BREED	LIVESTOCK	PET	TEAM
BURDEN	LOAD	PLOW	TRANSPORT
CART	MALE	PULL	WAGON
DOMESTICATED	MANE	RIDE	WORK
EARS	MARE	SADDLE	

Solution on page 272

Rodents

```
J A W S C H A M S T E R U F
T S E N E H E Z A M O U S E
L R I I V Q I S A T T I C U
A L N M I G I P A E N I U G
M V F R T L W N M E C I M O
M O E E C A I F M U S S O P
A L S V U M S B I S N I M H
M E T A R I R L U L E K D E
H P A E T N O D I R T Y T R
T N T B S A S L A B R H E A
E X I J E N I P U C R O P T
E L O M D C C L E S A E W A
T G N A W G N I W E H C G I
H O L E R R I U Q S M A L L
```

ANIMAL	EYES	INFESTATION	PORCUPINE
ATTIC	FILTH	JAWS	POSSUM
BEAVER	FUR	LAB	RAT
BURROW	GERBIL	MAMMAL	SMALL
CHEWING	GNAW	MAZE	SQUIRREL
CHIPMUNK	GOPHER	MICE	TAIL
DESTRUCTIVE	GUINEA PIG	MOLE	TEETH
DIRTY	HAMSTER	MOUSE	VERMIN
DISEASE	HOLE	NEST	VOLE
EXTERMINATOR	INCISORS	PET	WEASEL

Solution on page 272

Eagles

```
C V R B P G Y K S W I L D T
S I T O N P V G N S H S I F
O N W O R B N K E Y B I R D
A E R A C I O A D M K S T D
R T H H W S L E L B I P A E
S D G U D L A B O O T E D R
H G L N E S T M G L H C X E
E R O T P A R K E Y C I E G
N X M E G R A L V R O E R N
H O T R E H T A E F I S U A
R A C I T S E J A M N C T D
R S W L N H L A N O I T A N
G U N K A C Y L F R V C N E
S Y T S A F T R E E Y E T N
```

AMERICA	EYE	HUNTER	SOAR
BALD	FALCON	LARGE	SPECIES
BEAK	FAST	MAJESTIC	STRONG
BIRD	FEATHER	MASCOT	SYMBOL
BOOTED	FISH	NATIONAL	TALON
BROWN	FLY	NATURE	TREE
COIN	GOLDEN	NEST	USA
EGG	HARPY	POWER	WHITE
ENDANGERED	HAWK	RAPTOR	WILD
EXTINCT	HEAVY HEAD	SKY	WINGS

Solution on page 272

Golden Retriever

```
Z D Y A N I M A L F E T C H
V T A O C I G H M N L E T A
J G D O G T H A I D A X R I
T O H U N T I N G N Y E A R
X L I X G Z A V D I O R I G
L D U D E C S S E K L C N Z
E M E T N R S P O R T I N G
A H U U T E O L U H M S T A
S C F P L T I L C O K E K Y
H Y W T E A P R O T E C T L
R P E A T W A R F C N F F I
E P B A L E G X T X N J O M
D U C K S K C I R T E F S A
O P A T U D S Y E L L O W F
```

ACTIVE	EXERCISE	HUNTING	SHED
AGILITY	FAMILY	KENNEL	SIT
AKC	FETCH	KIND	SOFT
ANIMAL	FRIEND	LEASH	SPORTING
CANINE	FUN	LOYAL	TAIL
COAT	GENTLE	PET	TRAIN
COLOR	GOLD	PROTECT	TRICKS
CUTE	GROOMING	PUPPY	WALK
DOG	GUIDE	RED	WATER
DUCKS	HAIR	SEARCH	YELLOW

Solution on page 272

Photosynthesis

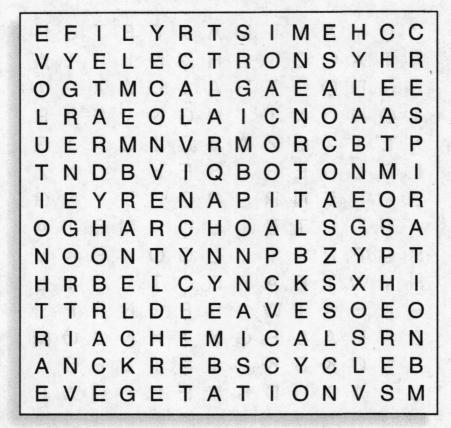

```
E F I L Y R T S I M E H C C
V Y E L E C T R O N S Y H R
O G T M C A L G A E A L E E
L R A E O L A I C N O A A S
U E R M N V R M O R C B T P
T N D B V I Q B O T O N M I
I E Y R E N A P I T A E O R
O G H A R C H O A L S G S A
N O O N T Y N N P B Z Y P T
H R B E L C Y N C K S X H I
T T R L D L E A V E S O E O
R I A C H E M I C A L S R N
A N C K R E B S C Y C L E B
E V E G E T A T I O N V S M
```

ABSORB	CHLOROPHYLL	LIFE
AIR	CONVERT	MEMBRANE
ALGAE	CYANOBACTERIA	NITROGEN
ATMOSPHERE	EARTH	OXYGEN
BOTANY	ELECTRONS	REACTION
CALVIN CYCLE	ENERGY	RESPIRATION
CARBOHYDRATE	EVOLUTION	STOMA
CELLS	GREEN PLANTS	VEGETATION
CHEMICALS	KREBS CYCLE	
CHEMISTRY	LEAVES	

Solution on page 273

Kangaroos

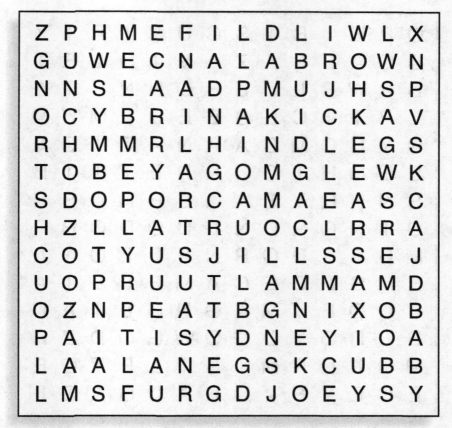

```
Z P H M E F I L D L I W L X
G U W E C N A L A B R O W N
N N S L A A D P M U J H S P
O C Y B R I N A K I C K A V
R H M M R L H I N D L E G S
T O B E Y A G O M G L E W K
S D O P O R C A M A E A S C
H Z L L A T R U O C L R R A
C O T Y U S J I L L S S E J
U O P R U U T L A M M A M D
O Z N P E A T B G N I X O B
P A I T I S Y D N E Y I O A
L A A L A N E G S K C U B B
L M S F U R G D J O E Y S Y
```

ANIMALS	DESERT	JILLS	POUCH
AUSTRALIAN	EARS	JOEYS	PUNCH
BABY	EMBLEM	JUMP	STRONG
BALANCE	ENDANGERED	KICK	SYDNEY
BOOMERS	FAST	LEAP	SYMBOL
BOXING	FUR	MACROPODS	TAILS
BROWN	GRAY	MAMMAL	TALL
BUCKS	HIND LEGS	MARSUPIAL	WALLABY
CARRY	HOPPING	MATE	WILDLIFE
COURT	JACKS	NOCTURNAL	ZOO

Solution on page 273

All Kinds of Flowers

```
Q P H I B I S C U S I R I X
D O A E L A Z A V I O L E T
B P W B L U E B O N N E T A
L P T I C K S E E D P M U M
O Y H O M C A R N A T I O N
S E O H T O O R R E T T I B
S N R Q Y S A G E B R U S H
O I N O R D N E D O D O H R
M B E E D O R N E D L O G L
E M S P G E C A M E L L I A
L U O E V M A G N O L I A U
B L R O Y D O O W G O D Z R
M O L N R M I S T L E T O E
E C E Y F L O R A U G A S L
```

AZALEA	FLORA	OREGON GRAPE
BITTERROOT	GOLDENROD	PEONY
BLOSSOM	HAWTHORN	POPPY
BLUEBONNET	HIBISCUS	RHODODENDRON
CAMELLIA	HYDRANGEA	ROSE
CARNATION	IRIS	SAGEBRUSH
CLOVER	LAUREL	SAGUARO
COLUMBINE	MAGNOLIA	TICKSEED
DOGWOOD	MISTLETOE	VIOLET
EMBLEM	MUM	

Solution on page 273

Organic Food

```
C E R T I F I E D X P W A M
S O G F V E G E T A B L E S
A T N G R G N I N E D R A G
T D O V S U B P O P U L A R
S F S R E Z I L I T R E F R
D O A U E N O T L T A S T E
O C O R N S T U S O E P V M
O K L I M Y C I V N C I E U
F N U T R I T I O U S A D S
E N V I R O N M E N T A L N
L W A G L E R G E F A S X O
O D A I E O B P Y I E L D C
H A O R H C X H E A L T H Y
W S G S R E M R A F R E S H
```

AGRICULTURE	EGGS	GREEN	SOIL
BIO	ENVIRONMENTAL	HEALTHY	STORES
CERTIFIED	EXPENSIVE	HORMONES	TASTE
CONSUMER	FARMERS	LOCAL	USDA
CONVENTIONAL	FARMING	MEAT	VEGETABLES
CORN	FERTILIZERS	MILK	WHOLE FOODS
DAIRY	FRESH	NUTRITIOUS	YIELD
DIET	FRUITS	POPULAR	
ECO	GARDENING	SAFE	

Solution on page 273

Buds

```
K L S Y L A C S P R I N G F
Q L P M I X E D T R E E D D
C A R L M N E E R G B E S P
N M O T A V P G G L K U A L
A S U A E N A I O A O L L B
T C T L C R T O N I B A E R
U O O N D C M Z T X T B T A
R P O E A E E I F E N G A N
E E N H S M T S N L K N C C
F M S O S N R T S A O E I H
I A R T E G R O W O L W L A
L N E V I T C U D O R P E R
H M D L Y N A T O B P Y D R
H A I R Y Y G O L O O Z U P
```

ACCESSORY	GARDEN	NATURE	SMALL
ADVENTITIOUS	GREEN	NEW	SPRING
BLOOM	GROW	NIP	SPROUT
BOTANY	HAIRY	PAL	STEM
BRANCH	LATENT	PLANT	TERMINAL
CABBAGE	LEAF	REPRODUCTIVE	TREE
DELICATE	LIFE	RESTING	ZOOLOGY
DEVELOP	MIXED	ROSE	
DORMANT	NAKED	SCALY	
FLOWER	NAME	SHOOT	

Solution on page 274

CHAPTER 8

BUSINESS

Business People

```
T S A M W A L T O N M P E S
A J C P E N N E Y A A A S E
R E L L E F E K C O R U U R
M R E H S I F A S L Y L O G
A H E I N Z F P A S K A H E
N O S I L L E Y R R A L G Y
D J P M O R G A N N Y L N B
H H C S U B D K O A A E I R
A S O Z E B I C F M S N T I
M G R R U T V W F T H B S N
M O K S S U A R T S I V E L
E U Y F O R D G J A Y W W K
R L A R R Y P A G E T T Y V
M D R O T H S C H I L D O W
```

ARMAND HAMMER	GETTY	PAUL ALLEN
BEZOS	GOULD	RAY KROC
BUSCH	HEINZ	ROCKEFELLER
DAVID GEFFEN	J C PENNEY	ROTHSCHILD
DOW	J P MORGAN	SAM WALTON
EASTMAN	LARRY ELLISON	SARNOFF
FISHER	LARRY PAGE	SERGEY BRIN
FORD	LEVI STRAUSS	SLOAN
GATES	MARY KAY ASH	WESTINGHOUSE

Solution on page 274

Nike, Inc.

```
E N O T R E V A E B R A N D
R N T F F O O T B A L L R R
O S A A T I O D T S U J A O
T S E M P T R A C K G E E G
S E M O R P R F D E W R W O
R D C U H E A U A T R S S L
O D L S G S W R O B E E T Y
S O O I H T G O E A T Y R M
N G T G O L F N B L A S O P
O T H G I N K P I L I H P I
P A I R J O R D A N L N S C
S D N A L T R O P D N I E S
Y B G C O M P A N Y S U B D
O M A N U F A C T U R E R S
```

ADS
AIR JORDAN
APPAREL
BASKETBALL
BEAVERTON
BILL BOWERMAN
BRAND
CLOTHING
COMPANY
FAMOUS

FOOTBALL
FOOTWEAR
GEAR
GODDESS
GOLF
JERSEYS
JUST DO IT
LINE
LOGO
MANUFACTURER

OLYMPICS
PHILIP KNIGHT
PORTLAND
RETAIL
RUNNING SHOES
SPONSORS
SPORTSWEAR
STORE
TIGER
TRACK

Solution on page 274

Buy a Mercedes

```
L V P O W E R F U L D S B Q
D D N H A B O T U A E S U X
T R A G T T U T S N A A S E
E L A I C O N I C O L L E L
C V E K M E F A S I E C S C
O O I S C L I W T T R H T I
A G U T E A E Y E A S Y U H
C N O P A I P R Z N H B D E
H I P L E V D Y B R I R E V
E C N A M R O F R E P I B S
S A G E R M A N Y T N D A P
T R A D I T I O N N J Z K E
W S C O N V E R T I B L E E
M E R C E D E S R E V I R D
```

AUTOBAHN	DRIVER	PERFORMANCE
BUSES	GERMANY	POWERFUL
CARS	HYBRID	QUALITY
CLASS	ICONIC	RACING
COACHES	INNOVATIVE	SAFE
CONVERTIBLE	INTERNATIONAL	SPEED
COUPE	LOGO	STUDEBAKER
DAIMLER BENZ	MERCEDES	STUTTGART
DEALERSHIP	NEW	TRADITION
DIESEL	PACKARD	VEHICLE

Solution on page 274

The Wall Street Journal

```
S N E W S T N E V E N N L E
C K C O T S N A T I O N A L
I O O D R N F I C I I Z N C
T F N S O B S Q T Y T C R I
I R O S P B U P W A A O U T
L E M B E O I L A N L M O R
O Z Y W R R R X L A U M J A
P T P R C O V T L L C O S W
A I U S E R K A S Y R D E R
G L B B O V S E T S I I C I
E U L T O W I S R I C T R T
S P I N K N U L E S V I U E
M D S S R E D A E R B E O R
E C H A R T S S T D P S S S
```

ANALYSIS	ECONOMY	PULITZER
ARTICLE	EDITOR	READERS
BONDS	EVENTS	REPORTS
BROKERS	INK	SOURCES
BULL	JOURNAL	SPORTS
CHARTS	NATIONAL	STOCK
CIRCULATION	NEWS	SUBSCRIPTION
COMMODITIES	PAGES	WALL STREET
CONSERVATIVE	POLITICS	WEBSITE
DELIVERY	PRESS	WRITERS
DOW	PUBLISH	

Solution on page 275

Currency Around the World

```
C S H S A C C R V A L U E A
T A T P E Q K R M R E T O N
Z B R O U F O R E X K M H E
E X O U R Y A P D D C O I N
Z S W N O E P B I R I E N D
D Z S D O O G B U Y N T N G
I K A P C V O P M G O L D T
M N P Z H R E V L I S A C A
E A X Q A E J M T H T C W I
S B R L N L O Y N L N O X F
N L L K G N N P I A I L Y R
A O L T E N D E R G M R R A
D A I Y E T I F P E D A R T
E N B P E S O S E L L H K E
```

BANK	DOLLAR	MARKET	PRINT
BILL	EURO	MEDIUM	RATE
BUY	FIAT	MINT	RUPEE
CASH	FOREX	MONEY	SELL
CENT	FRANC	NICKEL	SILVER
CHANGE	GOLD	NOTE	STORE
COIN	GOODS	PAY	TENDER
COPPER	LEGAL	PENNY	TRADE
CREDIT	LOAN	PESO	VALUE
DIME	LOCAL	POUND	WORTH

Solution on page 275

Credit Cards

```
Y T F E H T Y F Y O T Y M W
I E T F R U L N R X G T Z N
K K N A B O A E K A B N A B
E C U O A P C W G C U M S U
C I O N M N X S C R E D I T
X Q C O A E B O W E A H V K
F O C L S R E B M U N H C Y
N L A R W U N G I S R N C M
G B U S A C I P N S P E N D
T P H O L E L I M I T R L B
R O X F L S N N T Y H O I C
P G T R E P O R T B G T A N
A O R A T E S W I P E S D D
E L B I L L L G H L H D O Y
```

ACCOUNT	CREDIT	NAME	SHOP
APR	DEBT	NUMBER	SIGN
BALANCE	FEE	ONLINE	SPEND
BANK	FRAUD	OWE	STORE
BILL	GOLD	PIN	SWIPE
BUY	ISSUER	PURSE	THEFT
CASH	LIMIT	RATES	THIN
CHARGE	LOAN	REPORT	TOTAL
CHECK	LOGO	SCORE	VISA
COMPANY	MONEY	SECURE	WALLET

Solution on page 275

Bill Gates

```
S T N E M T S E V N I Q R R
H E N T R E P R E N E U R B
S L T O Y N A P M O C Y I T
P T M A R I C H M A N L T W
R T O Z G F C I B M L I E A
O A N C M A I L L I W M C S
G E E R K B D A O E C A H H
R S Y L A I T N E U L F N I
A F O U N D A T I O N T O N
M N A M R I A H C L P R L G
M A H A R V A R D D E A O T
I R E E R A C O F O O M G O
N O I T A R O P R O C S Y N
G A U T H O R Y T I R A H C
```

AUTHOR	ENTREPRENEUR	PHILANTHROPY
BILLIONAIRE	FAMILY	PROGRAMMING
CAREER	FOUNDATION	RICH MAN
CEO	HARVARD	SEATTLE
CHAIRMAN	IBM	SMART
CHARITY	INFLUENTIAL	STOCK
COMPANY	INVESTMENTS	TECHNOLOGY
CORPORATION	MELINDA GATES	WASHINGTON
DOS	MONEY	WILLIAM

Solution on page 275

Warren Buffett

```
G E N E R O U S D N O B H Y
J P H I L A N T H R O P Y N
S R I C H A I R M A N B M T
T W A L L S T R E E T O O T
O L A I T N E U L F N I N E
C G E I C O D D S E B R O F
K N B O O K S P Y J O E C F
M I N V E S T M E N T S E U
A D A L E C A R N E G I E B
R A R X L N T R E W O P L N
K R A S A G E O F O M A H A
E T O G A K S A R B E N P S
T T E F F U B E I S U S F U
H R S R E D L O H E R A H S
```

BONDS	INFLUENTIAL	STOCK MARKET
BOOKS	INVESTMENTS	SUSAN BUFFETT
CEO	MONEY MANAGER	SUSIE BUFFETT
CHAIRMAN	NEBRASKA	TAXES
DALE CARNEGIE	PHILANTHROPY	TRADING
ECONOMY	POWER	UNITED STATES
FORBES	RICH	WALL STREET
GEICO	SAGE OF OMAHA	
GENEROUS	SHAREHOLDERS	

Solution on page 276

Delivery Service

```
T K C U R T S L A U N D R Y
H K P O V R A R A Y Q S A K
G S U A E A E D A T H D Z R
I T P W C V I X D I S O Z O
E E O R I K O R P R L O I W
R L C R O B A B L O E G P T
F U D O V D U G Q I Y S G E
L D C O N S U M E R N N S N
E E A O I T A C E P I E P R
R H V N U I E V T K N X E O
O C E A L R I N C S I G C A
T S F V R L I A T C E R I D
S P S U E T P E U S E A A S
R O O D X S S E R P X E L C
```

ADDRESS	DOOR	PACKAGE	SEA
AIRLINE	DRIVER	PACKING	SHIP
BOX	EXPRESS	PIZZA	SIGN
BUSINESS	FLOWERS	POSTAL	SPECIAL
CAR	FREIGHT	PRIORITY	STORE
CONSUMER	GOODS	PRODUCTS	TRAVEL
CONTENTS	INVOICE	RAIL	TRUCK
COURIER	LAUNDRY	ROADS	UPS
DELIVERY	MAIL	ROUTE	USPS
DIRECT	NETWORK	SCHEDULE	VAN

Solution on page 276

MGM

```
D W S R O T C E R I D D S N
S I A E C N E I C S K N E A
G Z S A M E R I C A N A L O
N A C T S M L I F U C L E L
I R O A R N S R A T S R G S
D D M E D I A C O M P A N Y
L O C J Z A B R B P V G A R
O F A C U T S U H N I Y S R
H O S C A R S T T Z D D O A
M Z T A L E N T N I E U L H
G T H E A T E R X E O J I Y
M R E G A N E D L O G N O N
K I R K K E R K O R I A N O
F E L B A G K R A L C G T S
```

ACTORS	GOLDEN AGE	ROAR
AGENTS	HARRY SLOAN	SCIENCE
AMERICAN	JUDY GARLAND	SONY
CLARK GABLE	KIRK KERKORIAN	STARS
COMCAST	LION	TALENT
DIRECTORS	LOS ANGELES	THEATER
DISTRIBUTION	MEDIA COMPANY	VIDEO
ENTERTAINMENT	MGM HOLDINGS	WIZARD OF OZ
FILMS	OSCARS	

Solution on page 276

Packaging

```
I S H I P R I N T S E L A S
H F M C R E C Y C L E N B E
T C E T O R P I S E G U L A
L F O O D W R M C L S A A L
A U M H U R E A O I T J B E
E N I H C A M T N G I S E D
H F A R T P U E T A C L L E
Y T E F A S S R E R K I G T
M A I L R S N I N F E A N H
E U L G H E O A T P R T I G
Y N A P M O C L S O E E T I
I P L A S T I C T X V R I E
A I N T F I G S T S O C R W
D K C A P A D D I N G B W N
```

ART	DISPLAY	MATERIAL	SAFETY
BAG	FOOD	NAME	SALE
BOX	FRAGILE	PACK	SEALED
BUSINESS	GIFT	PADDING	SHIP
CAN	GLUE	PLASTIC	STICKER
COMPANY	HEALTH	PRINT	STORAGE
CONSUMER	LABEL	PRODUCT	TEXT
CONTENTS	LID	PROTECT	WEIGHT
COSTS	MACHINE	RECYCLE	WRAP
DESIGN	MAIL	RETAIL	WRITING

Solution on page 276

Donald Trump

```
N S E L P A M A L R A M U J
B B D I V O R C E E R I C H
C A B I L L I O N A I R E A
T N P E R S O N A L I T Y Z
H K T L H D S S C I M A D A
E R E A L E S T A T E J A L
D U L S A I E R S Y L M U P
O P E V U R C U I S A A G P
N T V E T R C C N H N H H M
A C I G H A U T O O I A T U
L Y S A O M S I S W A L E R
D R I S R E W O T P M U R T
F L O G I V A N A T R U M P
S G N I D L I U B O O K S U
```

AUTHOR	GOLF	REALITY SHOW
BANKRUPTCY	IVANA TRUMP	RICH
BILLIONAIRE	LAS VEGAS	SUCCESS
BOOKS	MARLA MAPLES	TAJ MAHAL
BUILDINGS	MARRIED	TELEVISION
CASINOS	MELANIA	THE DONALD
CONSTRUCTION	NBC	TRUMP PLAZA
DAUGHTER	PERSONALITY	TRUMP TOWERS
DIVORCE	REAL ESTATE	

Solution on page 277

Google Inc.

```
L B A U C O M P U T E R S H
D R O F N A T S E O E C S C
P O P U L A R S G G I L E R
S W A S W E N X D T E I N A
E S G I Y E N E Y N G N I E
T E E F S S L L L U A K S S
E R R D I W A P I O P S U E
N U A F O N E E A C Y O B R
R T N N A V D L M C R F E E
E A K L I A M G E A R T A S
T E C H N O L O G Y A W P U
N F C A I N R O F I L A C L
I R A N K I N G Q U E R Y T
A S D R O W D A N S W E R S
```

ACCOUNT	E MAIL	PAGERANK
ADSENSE	FEATURES	POPULAR
ADWORDS	FIND	QUERY
ANALYTICS	FREE	RANKING
ANSWERS	GMAIL	RESEARCH
ARCHIVE	GOOGLEPLEX	RESULTS
BROWSER	INTERNET	SOFTWARE
BUSINESS	KNOWLEDGE	STANFORD
CALIFORNIA	LARRY PAGE	TECHNOLOGY
COMPUTERS	LINKS	
EASY	NEWS	

Solution on page 277

Business Trade

```
O V E C O N O M Y H K P L S
G N B R S F R E E T R A D E
R O U E H S E I R T N U O C
A I Y T I D O M M O C D I I
B T I R P B U S I N E S S P
M A N A Y R A T E N O M E S
E I G B T N A H C R E M U R
S T N E M N R E V O G B L E
T O C U R R E N C Y S Z A D
O G O E D A R T R I A F V R
C E T C A P R O D U C T S O
K N W S E R V I C E S J O B
I C C O M M E R C E C I R P
R O U T E S E A R N I N G W
```

BARTER	EMBARGO	PRICE
BORDERS	FAIR TRADE	PRODUCTS
BUSINESS	FREE TRADE	ROUTES
BUYING	GOVERNMENTS	SERVICES
COMMERCE	INTERNATIONAL	SHIP
COMMODITY	JOB	SPICES
COUNTRIES	MERCHANT	STOCK
CURRENCY	MONETARY	SUBSIDIES
EARNING	NEGOTIATION	VALUE
ECONOMY	PACT	WTO

Solution on page 277

The Petroleum Business

```
N E G O R T I N D U S T R Y
S T C U D O R P L A N T S R
E R E F I N I N G N O X X E
V G T S A E E L D D I M E N
R A D E A L A S K A T H R I
E S B A R R E L S P A Y O F
S O C R U D E O I L R D H E
E L J T D P O P E C O R S R
R I A H D I E S E L L O F O
U N G N I L L I R D P G F C
S E N O I T C A R T X E O K
S L E N V I R O N M E N T O
I K E R O S E N E R G Y P I
A S C I T S A L P E T R O L
```

ALASKA	EXXON	PETROL
BARRELS	GASOLINE	PIPELINES
CRUDE OIL	HYDROGEN	PLANTS
DIESEL	INDUSTRY	PLASTICS
DRILLING	KEROSENE	PRODUCTS
EARTH	MIDDLE EAST	REFINERY
ENERGY	NATURAL GAS	REFINING
ENVIRONMENT	NITROGEN	RESERVES
EXPLORATION	OFFSHORE	ROCK OIL
EXTRACTION	OPEC	RUSSIA

Solution on page 277

CHAPTER 9

IN THE HOUSE

Door Handles

```
B R X S X H S U P S A R G W
P R H P I R G L T W I S T G
G U C H R O M E N E P O L F
T E L D N I P S S R H A E F
B L R L X R V I B C S Z V W
S E A M G L L A T S N I E I
J S G T S V C A C O S D R S
X O U A E K L P R Y N A T P
Q L E R S M S B C A M D R X
T C N E E S U O H K N M U B
T E T O R N A T E U N L U T
M U E L R E P P O C G O L D
C A R D O O R R O O M C B B
F L J N S B I H O E G K E Y
```

BACKSET	ENTER	KEY	PULL
BOLT	GERMS	KNOB	PUSH
BRASS	GLASS	LATCH	ROOM
BRONZE	GOLD	LEVER	ROUND
CAR	GRASP	LOCK	SCREWS
CHROME	GRIP	METAL	SHUT
CLOSE	HAND	OPEN	SILVER
COPPER	HOUSE	ORNATE	SPINDLE
DOOR	INSTALL	PASSAGE	TURN
DUMMY	JAM	PRIVACY	TWIST

Solution on page 278

Toy Shelf

```
E X E R C I S E S T O R Y S
R V S M B U I L D I N G T T
A I S A M T S I R H C N T E
H D N T P W M A Q L L I U P
S E G T Y T E F A S E H P O
E O B E E B C Y E K A T Y R
I G B L Y R H M A C R Y L P
R A E D U C A T I O N A L M
E M D C W G N C T L I L I U
T E Y A D A I T T B N P S J
T S B R S K C A J I G O L S
A G A S N I A R T M V G L Y
B O B C H I L D R E N E A O
B C H I L D H O O D P L B T
```

BABY	EDUCATIONAL	SAFETY
BALLS	EXERCISE	SANTA
BATTERIES	INTERACTIVE	SHARE
BLOCKS	JACKS	SILLY PUTTY
BOARD GAMES	JUMP ROPE	STORY
BUILDING	LEARNING	TEDDY BEAR
CARS	LEGO	TOYS
CHILDHOOD	MATTEL	TRAINS
CHILDREN	MECHANICAL	VIDEO GAME
CHRISTMAS	PETS	
CLAY	PLAYTHING	

Solution on page 278

Light a Candle

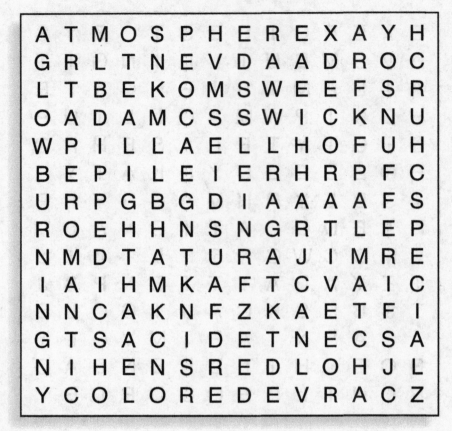

```
A T M O S P H E R E X A Y H
G R L T N E V D A A D R O C
L T B E K O M S W E E F S R
O A D A M C S S W I C K N U
W P I L L A E L L H O F U H
B E P I L E I E R H R P F C
U R P G B G D I A A A A F S
R O E H H N S N G R T L E P
N M D T A T U R A J I M R E
I A I H M K A F T C V A I C
N N C A K N F Z K A E T F I
G T S A C I D E T N E C S A
N I H E N S R E D L O H J L
Y C O L O R E D E V R A C Z
```

ADVENT	COLORED	HEAT	SMOKE
ATMOSPHERE	DECORATIVE	HOLDERS	SNUFFER
BEESWAX	DIPPED	JAR	SOY
BURNING	FIRE	LIGHTING	SPECIAL
CANDELABRA	FLICKER	MATCH	TAPER
CARVED	FRAGRANCE	MELT	TEA LIGHT
CHANDELIER	GLASS	PARAFFIN	WICK
CHRISTMAS	GLOW	ROMANTIC	
CHURCH	HANUKKAH	SCENTED	

Solution on page 278

Tables

```
T C C S K R O W Q R V G S W
D O O W F L G A P M A L V A
F F P V D L U D K M K T E S
A W R I A H C N E N I P L I
F R C S C L M T C A R D R D
O N S A J N A O I H T L E E
R R M D S L I K F M C S K R
M E D C I O R C F L K Q O K
A D N R E N I O O L W U P I
L O O N A C I T O F N A L R
I M D L I W H N A D F R A F
H I F O L D I N G P T E T G
M W Z J A X A N T I Q U E X
D O O F L A T H G I N L O W
```

ANTIQUE	END	METAL	PLATE
CARD	FLAT	MODERN	POKER
CHAIR	FOLDING	NIGHT	ROUND
CLOTH	FOOD	OAK	SET
COFFEE	FORMAL	OFFICE	SIDE
DESK	GAME	OUTDOOR	SOFA
DINING	GLASS	OVAL	SQUARE
DINNER	LAMP	PATIO	TOP
DRAWING	LEG	PICNIC	WOOD
EAT	LUNCH	PINE	WORK

Solution on page 278

Move the Furniture

```
P H C U O C F B M O D E R N
U E F U N C T I O N A L O D
L M U S P T F R E N C H R N
D O T M Q B R T O U A A R A
O H O Y O T O C S F W O I T
O D N T H O I A O E M L M S
W F S I S T R S R L H O K W
A E H L S P E A E D T C C C
L N E A E E T G N G E H H K
N I L U T R N E I T N A U S
U P V Q R I I V L E I U V E
T M E I N O A O C R B Q O D
J A S I N D O M E T A L U L
H L D E B G H D R O C E D E
```

ANTIQUE	DINING	LIVING	RECLINER
BED	DOOR	LOUNGE	ROOM
CABINET	DRAWER	METAL	SET
CHAIR	FRENCH	MIRROR	SHELVES
CHEST	FUNCTIONAL	MODERN	SIT
COMFORT	FUTON	MOVE	SOFA
COUCH	HOME	PERIOD	STAND
CUPBOARD	INTERIOR	PINE	STOOL
DECOR	LAMP	PLASTIC	WALNUT
DESK	LEG	QUALITY	WOOD

Solution on page 279

Dishwasher

```
Z S T O P L A T E L S I N K
K Z D E V I C E F I N K X R
D T M S S Q H C R M O U U O
C O A A B U R C S F O O D F
T L O E I I D K K K C A T S
D D O R H D L S C S Y C O I
K L D G A T Y A M L R L S W
H A O L W M R P O W D E R P
L D O A Y H S I D O S A A U
R D T S D A P I E B E N Y W
J E T S A F R F R S S F A L
R M M A E T S P N O I S E A
R H Z I Y D U I S L H O T F
E Y B X T C R I L V N F H E
```

BOWLS	FILL	MAYTAG	SCRUB
CLEAN	FOOD	MODERN	SINK
CLOG	FORK	NOISE	SOAK
CUP	GLASS	PANS	SPRAY
DEVICE	GREASE	PLATE	STACK
DIRTY	HEAT	POTS	STEAM
DISH	HOT	POWDER	SUDS
DOOR	KNIFE	RACK	TIMER
DRY	LIQUID	RINSE	WASH
FAST	LOAD	SCOUR	WATER

Solution on page 279

Interior Design

```
W T N I A P E M E H T V G Z
A U T R O L O C L I E N T S
L O O H C S R O R R I M E X
L Y R O O M P I L L O W S D
P A T T E R N O I H S A F X
H L C S P A C E S R I A H C
O T E F O E C N A L A B N W
M P J L E F I X T U R E S P
E E O O Y A A E R C H F B E
L C R O T T T H O C A O D R
I N P R A A S U T B O P N I
T O U B E G C I R K J L E O
R C L R U H K I S E P A R D
A E C R L E C I F F O N T C
```

ART	CURTAINS	LAYOUT	RUG
BALANCE	DEN	MIRRORS	SCHOOL
BOOKS	DRAPES	OFFICE	SOFA
CEILING	FABRIC	PAINT	SPACE
CHAIRS	FASHION	PATTERN	STYLE
CLIENTS	FEATURE	PERIOD	TABLE
COLOR	FIXTURES	PILLOWS	THEME
CONCEPT	FLOOR	PLAN	TILE
COUCH	HOME	PROJECT	TREND
CREATE	KITCHEN	ROOM	WALL

Solution on page 279

Carpets

```
E X P E N S I V E U L G D D
L M R O O D T U O F I B E R
I I B S L L O R C I T A T S
P P P R H Y R T S E P A T H
N A E O O T E X T I L E O A
O D R L U I T S U D P M N G
I D S O S L D Y T A E G K G
H I I C E I Q E T E L N L G
S N A P R B T T R I R I O R
U G N I N A E L C Y S D O O
C O N S T R U C T I O N P U
N O L Y N U E V A E W I E N
N G I S E D R E B R E B D D
F K C I H T U F T E D Y X I
```

BERBER	EMBROIDERY	NYLON	ROLL
BINDING	EXPENSIVE	OUTDOOR	SHAG
CLEANING	FIBER	PADDING	STATIC
COLORS	GLUE	PATTERNS	TAPESTRY
CONSTRUCTION	GROUND	PERSIAN	TEXTILE
CUSHION	HOME	PETS	THICK
DENSITY	HOUSE	PILE	TUFTED
DESIGN	KNOTTED	POLYESTER	WEAVE
DURABILITY	LOOPED	RED	
DUST	NAP	RIP	

Solution on page 279

Bedbugs Are Here

```
B E D D I N G U B M B E S L
T R A V E L I N G A L R S A
S H N N S W Y K E T O U N V
L L G O L A N W S T O T O O
O E E I E R I I A R D I C E
R L R T T C T N E E S N T S
T U O A O P I G S S U R U U
N S U T H M E L I S C U R O
O I S S R U J E D E K F N L
C V R E B A T S L S I L A L
T E T F P H O S T S N A L L
S X G N I P E E L S G T V A
E P C I P O C S O R C I M W
P A R A S I T I C O V E R S
```

BATS	FLAT	OVAL
BEDDING	FURNITURE	PARASITIC
BLOODSUCKING	HOSTS	PEST CONTROL
BUG	HOTELS	SKIN
COVERS	INFESTATION	SLEEP TIGHT
CRAWL	LICE	SLEEPING
DANGEROUS	MATTRESSES	TINY
DISEASE	MICROSCOPIC	TRAVELING
ELUSIVE	MOTELS	WALL LOUSE
EXTERMINATORS	NOCTURNAL	WINGLESS

Solution on page 280

Light Fixtures

```
Q J S W Q T R A L O S H H D
Q L A M P O T E K C O S W E
M G L O W R C O R D H I Y X
O I W B G C N E G O L A H I
O E S U O H W G N I T T I F
R F L L U S G N I G N A H N
C P L B T D E L L P K S M O
P B A O D F C K I T C H E N
I S W M O U N T E D A S T R
R R W T O D O G C L R T A E
T H G I R B C L I C T T L T
S M F M T W S G R S N A F N
W I R E U C H T C X E W H A
C D A R K T H G I N W D B L
```

BRIGHT	FIXED	LIGHT	SOCKET
BULB	FLOOD	METAL	SOLAR
CEILING	GLOW	MOUNTED	STRIP
CHAIN	HALOGEN	NIGHT	SWITCH
CORD	HANGING	OUTDOOR	TIMER
DARK	HOUSE	PLUG	TORCH
DESIGN	KITCHEN	POWER	TRACK
DIM	LAMP	ROOM	WALL
FAN	LANTERN	SCONCE	WATTS
FITTING	LED	SCREWS	WIRE

Solution on page 280

Dust

```
S G M R O A D F L I G W A S
R C N J S T B L K R A T S A
J D A H E S U O H T R C W M
G R E B I F G O E S E U T O
Q S L B G A I R M M K W Y L
E W C P R Z D E O O W I N D
W E O D O I A H G U O N N B
T E V C I M S O C D N R U X
O P E L I N T R E S E D B X
U B R O S J H G L T I L S Q
E C W T T M M H T R A E P C
T S O H E L A A T Y R D P J
I R P A P I M L E Y A I S D
M S O I L F H R L D V K R A
```

AIR	DEBRIS	HOUSE	ROAD
ASHES	DESERT	LAYER	SAW
ASTHMA	DIRT	LINT	SKIN
BROOM	DRY	MATTER	SMALL
BUNNY	EARTH	MITE	SOIL
CLEAN	FIBER	MOP	STAR
CLOTH	FILM	OLD	STORM
COAL	FLOOR	PETS	SWEEP
COSMIC	GROUND	PLEDGE	WATER
COVER	HOME	RAG	WIND

Solution on page 280

Laundry

```
L Y O M R A W A T E R K T T
L G L R G N A H B G A B I T
N L C I S U H C I Z T U D F
I H E O N I P S H T S R E M
A J C M I E E H A O E C I F
T K O O S N E S N I R S R D
S D L U T A E H A M P E R R
D C O N P T P R E S S H Q Y
U H R D A R O K B H D T E W
S N P E N I G N I D L O F E
N A P L T H V H C A E L B W
O E B I S S E E N I H C A M
R L L O A D N B R Q W S G T
I C X S O A K C G Q H N F H
```

BAG	FOLDING	PANTS	SPIN
BLEACH	FRESH	PRESS	STAIN
CHORE	HAMPER	REPEAT	SUDS
CLEAN	HANG	RINSE	SUIT
CLOTHES	HEAT	SCRUB	TIDE
COIN	HOUSE	SHIRT	WARM
COLOR	IRON	SMELL	WASH
COTTON	LINE	SOAK	WATER
DIRT	LOAD	SOCKS	WET
DRY	MACHINE	SOILED	WHITES

Solution on page 280

Bed

```
O F M U S R B D T V G P X S
V L U O V J A E Y C O T P R
W M F F O P S Z R A I L S R
U T C E D R E A M N W O D F
K W A C U D D L E O B T M W
Z W L G V L F R L P S I Z E
G A N E E U Q L E Y E R R I
T T O M T L I U Q L J E R C
O E A O Y P B R A S S D L T
O R N W A R M U L N N I K S
F E E S H E E T O K I N G O
O S N L T H G I N D P W L P
A T I A O L L U F B O S T A
M E L Y X O B L H V A U P N
```

BASE	DOWN	LINEN	REST
BOX	DREAM	METAL	ROOM
BRASS	DUVET	NAP	SHEET
BUNK	FOAM	NIGHT	SIZE
CANOPY	FOOT	PAD	SLEEP
COT	FRAME	PILLOW	SOFT
CRADLE	FULL	POST	TIRED
CRIB	FUTON	QUEEN	TWIN
CUDDLE	KING	QUILT	WARM
DOUBLE	LAY	RAILS	WATER

Solution on page 281

Sewing Machine

```
T O O F L E V E R E P P I Z
H O B B Y A M K K E T I C I
R E G N I S D E L D E E N G
E L A N T P T E N G X C T Z
A Q A I I A C J P D T H K A
D N T I I T D A R N I N G G
F C O L R T S M B M L N B U
H A O I M E H A B I E K G I
F R C S S R T L B L N D R D
P A N T S N E A D O I E H E
N I B B O B E A M O H S T Y
S S E R D R E T M P C I O A
R E P A I R Y W E S A G L R
Q U I L T C R O T O M N C N
```

BASTING	FOOT	NEEDLE	STITCH
BOBBIN	GUIDE	PANTS	TAILOR
CABINET	HEM	PATTERN	TENSION
CLOTH	HOBBY	PEDAL	TEXTILE
DARNING	JAM	PIN	THIMBLE
DESIGN	LEVER	QUILT	THREAD
DRESS	MACHINE	REPAIR	TREADLE
ELECTRIC	MATERIAL	SEW	YARN
FABRIC	MENDING	SINGER	ZIGZAG
FACTORY	MOTOR	SPOOL	ZIPPER

Solution on page 281

Toaster

```
W S T O V E N T Y D O O F S
I M U F F I N B R E A D M A
R Q G N I N R O M O D E L K
E O W N B G E S A T D S C R
T B S A I E U H M R K I O A
T H U N F T A B C A R G N D
U S O R E F T M C T L N V G
B R O W N S L E C P I L E E
O C H R O M E E S O N K Y T
R R R H F K L N H P O O O O
W W E U R E T N U O C K R A
M A Q V M F D R O C T O L S
T R Y H E B A G E L I G H T
E M C O I L S L I C E N O D
```

BAGEL	COUNTER	HEAT	SENSOR
BREAD	CRUMBS	HOT	SETTING
BROWN	DARK	KITCHEN	SLICE
BURN	DEFROST	LEVER	SLOT
BUTTER	DESIGN	LIGHT	SMALL
CHROME	DING	MODEL	SUNBEAM
COILS	DONE	MORNING	TOAST
CONVEYOR	ELECTRIC	MUFFIN	WAFFLE
COOK	FOOD	OVEN	WARM
CORD	GIFT	POP TART	WIRE

Solution on page 281

CHAPTER 10

JUST FOR FUN

Amusement Arcade

```
T O L S S C R E E N A R C Y
I E Q R I A F C K P N D C I
C M T I C Z G N I T O O H S
K A C I S U M A C H I N E S
E G N E L L A H C N T K G P
T G O D N T L C U S C E Q L
S M B K Y T N F D S A Y R A
T O K E N A I R H O C K E Y
Y N N E P I A P T U Z O T A
N E R D L I H C E N T N R W
S Y O T L A R C A D E G A D
B O W L I N G Z A S E L U I
S K I L L A B N I P C E Q M
C B V E N U E C P R I Z E S
```

ACTION	CLAW	MUSIC	SHOOTING
AIR HOCKEY	COIN	PACHINKO	SKILL
ARCADE	CRANE	PENNY	SLOT
BILLIARDS	DONKEY KONG	PINBALL	SOUNDS
BOWLING	FAIR	PLAY	TICKETS
CANDY	FUN	PONG	TILT
CENTIPEDE	GAME	PRIZE	TOKEN
CHALLENGE	MACHINES	QUARTER	TOYS
CHANCE	MIDWAY	RACING	VENUE
CHILDREN	MONEY	SCREEN	

Solution on page 281

Water Balloons

```
W D R S O P S B D G S R O B
H D N U O R A D I G P O P O
N C B M O B L S P V A L V E
C W N M I A F O Q A I M A K
A H O E L T T A B Q R E E Y
J F Z R R T L K U H C T A C
S S Z Q H D E I Z C J N Y H
R R L W E T D G B N E I B O
Y X E T A L N E R U Y T W S
I T I B G P K C E A O H A E
O E S F B O N H A L T G R V
X K D U J U A A K H F I L L
A I I N B U R S T S F F I R
H K K D R O P E M N M B M J
```

AIM	FAUCET	LATEX	RUBBER
BATTLE	FIGHT	LAUNCH	SOAK
BOMB	FILL	LIQUID	SUMMER
BREAK	FIRE	LOB	TARGET
BURST	FUN	NOZZLE	THROW
BUST	GAME	PARTY	TIE
CATCH	HID	PLAY	TOY
CHASE	HOSE	POP	VALVE
DRENCH	JOKE	PRANK	WAR
DROP	KIDS	ROUND	WET

Solution on page 282

Fabled Unicorns

```
G G X F P I N K D R E A M S
R O R E F I E R C E M N E Y
E E A L A R I P S X A P D M
E T R T K A D Y E T G A I B
K N H N E R R N U I I G E O
L E I E A T A R L N C A V L
O I N G S M E M A C U N A D
R C O E T I H W M T A I L N
E N P S M Y S T I C A L D E
D A E H E R O F N E D L O G
T L O V E V U M A I D E N E
M Y T H O L O G I C A L L L
E U Q I N U H O R N E D I W
Y M H S E S R O H X Y R O W
```

ANCIENT	FREE	LOVE	PINK
ANIMAL	GENTLE	MAGIC	RHINO
ART	GOAT	MAIDEN	SPIRAL
BEAUTIFUL	GOLDEN	MANE	SYMBOL
DRAGON	GREEK	MEDIEVAL	TAIL
DREAMS	HOOVES	MYSTICAL	TAPESTRY
EXTINCT	HORNED	MYTHOLOGICAL	UNIQUE
FAKE	HORSES	NATURE	WHITE
FIERCE	LEGEND	ORYX	WILD
FOREHEAD	LORE	PAGAN	

Solution on page 282

Leisure

```
K R A L R E H T A E R B G K
N O O M Y E N O H N U K N D
T I M E O F F R O L I C I I
V E G E T A T I O N S A M V
E P A C S E T N L U R L A E
M A D S F A O A E T T S E R
I M A U E I W C M B H T R S
T U N R P A S T I M E G D I
E S C Y T I V I T S E F I O
E E I R E J U V E N A T E N
R M N T N E M I R R E M A G
F E G M N O I T A X A L E R
E N I L C E R Y P I C N I C
S T C A L M N E S S L E E P
```

AMUSEMENT	FROLIC	RECLINE
BREATHER	FUN	RECREATION
CALMNESS	GAME	REJUVENATE
DANCING	HONEYMOON	RELAXATION
DIVERSION	INACTIVITY	SLACK
DREAMING	LARK	SLEEP
EASE	MERRIMENT	SPARE TIME
ESCAPE	NIGHTLIFE	TIME OFF
FESTIVITY	PASTIME	VEGETATION
FREE TIME	PICNIC	

Solution on page 282

Spring Break Time

```
S S N B P G N I Y T R A P F
A U W E E I F R I E N D S L
D I N I E A R S Y O B V N O
C A R S M R C T R O S E R R
L O N F H S C H D A T N U I
U S C C A I U S T A B T B D
B E R E I R N I N O O U N A
S R E G A N E E T U W R U N
L I L S U N G L A S S E S O
A F A V O L L E Y B A L L T
D N X L O O P G E T A W A Y
N O I T A C A V C R A Z Y A
A B N L U G G A G E N U F D
S A G N I M M I W S L R I G
```

ADVENTURE	FRIENDS	SANDALS
AIRFARE	FUN	SUNBURN
BARS	GETAWAY	SUNGLASSES
BEACH TOWEL	GIRLS	SUNSCREEN
BONFIRES	LUGGAGE	SUNSHINE
BOYS	OCEAN	SWIMMING
CLUBS	PARTYING	SWIMSUITS
CRAZY	POOL	TAN
DANCING	RELAXING	TEENAGERS
DAYTONA	RESORT	VACATION
FLORIDA	ROAD TRIP	VOLLEYBALL

Solution on page 282

Dominoes

```
Z O Z X I H Y G R O Z Z O S
W T C I V O R Y A T N U O C
A H T A M J D L E M S J T A
R A I S S S O I F B E I B R
D I E T T T T M F A L L L D
K V I O E N S A E E U A O S
G U P C N I U F C U R U C E
S S A K D O P F T K B H K K
P N C H S P C I E L I F I C
I G K M A R B L E L A N N E
P I A E R O C S D C P V G D
L S P I N N E R E Z E P X S
A E T A B L E J Z U T S O E
Y D O M S N U M B E R S B T
```

BLACK	DOUBLES	MARBLE	SET
BLOCKING	DRAW	MATH	SPINNER
BOX	EFFECT	NUMBERS	SPOTS
CARDS	ENDS	PACK	STACKING
CHILDREN	FACE	PIECES	STOCK
COUNT	FALL	PIPS	SUITS
DECK	FAMILY	PLAY	TABLE
DESIGN	FUN	POINTS	TILE
DIE	GAME	RULES	TOPPLE
DOTS	IVORY	SCORE	WHITE

Solution on page 283

Funfair

```
N A C H O S L A M I N A A A A
T I B I H X E M A G Y M C U
P E O P L E S T C Y L U A A
S N U F E P H R H D I S R T
H E N T E R T A I N M E N T
O R C N H I O V N A A M I R
W D Y E W Z O E E C F E V A
A L C T S E B L R A K N A C
X I A P I Z Z A Y D C T L T
W H S F R I E D D O U G H I
O C T G R O U N D S L S U O
R O L L E R C O A S T E R N
K B E M F N R O C P O P N I
S G O D T O H L O O H C S W
```

AMUSEMENT	FAMILY	PIZZA
ANIMALS	FERRIS WHEEL	POPCORN
ATTRACTION	FRIED DOUGH	PRIZE
BOOTHS	FUN	ROLLER COASTER
BOUNCY CASTLE	GAME	SCHOOL
CANDY	GROUNDS	SHOW
CARNIVAL	HOT DOGS	SODA
CHILDREN	LUCK	TENT
ENTERTAINMENT	MACHINERY	TRAVEL
EXHIBIT	NACHOS	WAXWORKS
FAIR	PEOPLE	WIN

Solution on page 283

Winter Celebrations

```
M C A R O L S Y L I M A F T
U O Y E C I T S L O S V O R
S O F U N A I S R E P F O N
I K V S L E D D I N G M D O
C I D E R E P I P H A N Y I
N E W Y E A R H I N D U R T
H S E E F F O C S S V D A A
V A R E B M E C E D E L U R
J A N U A R Y D O Q N O R B
E Z S U I W A T S C T C B E
L N A F K R L I G H T S E L
V A N S A K S T F I G O F E
E W T P U S A M T S I R H C
S K A T I N G H C I T L E C
```

ADVENT	COOKIES	GIFTS	PARADES
BUDDHIST	DECEMBER	HANUKKAH	PERSIAN
CAROLS	ELVES	HINDU	ROMAN
CELEBRATION	EPIPHANY	HOT COCOA	SANTA
CELTIC	FAMILY	JANUARY	SKATING
CHRISTMAS	FEBRUARY	KWANZAA	SLEDDING
CIDER	FIRE	LIGHTS	SOLSTICE
COFFEE	FOOD	MUSIC	SUN
COLD	FUN	NEW YEAR	YULE

Solution on page 283

Waterslide

```
H R M O T C S E B U T Q M X
C T Y S I E S G K X Z A F A
A H W V P Q W U N I U M L T
B L O I E U I R B O D Y U L
P E E T S D M Y U H L S M S
T U R N S T I P L U N G E B
R P T I N U F R L I F F E D
A S O E R U S I E L M L S L
O L N O R P T N T M O A O I
G I B A L U T D L R M O F W
L P F A S T N O D P O U P A
F T S P E E D O A R E S S T
T H R I L L W R C H U T E E
E H Z E F N K C B K G Z P R
```

BIG	HOT	PUMP	SWIM
BODY	INDOOR	RAFT	TALL
BULLET	KIDS	RESORT	THRILL
CHUTE	LEISURE	RIDE	TUBE
DOWN	LINE	RUN	TUNNEL
FAMILY	LONG	SLIP	TURNS
FAST	LOOP	SPEED	TWIST
FLOW	PARK	SPLASH	WATER
FLUME	PLUNGE	STEEP	WET
FUN	POOL	SUMMER	WILD

Solution on page 283

Play Cards

```
I O F I O I X H O P D B D O
K H P F T U E L T I U S E W
M X R E N D B N S L A E D T
S G N I K L L A C E D E V R
O R E R I O P L A Y L C L I
D N E L U F L U S H D U R Q
U B U K B T B R I D G E R Y
T Y Q F O A E F N C K D C W
S V M K L P T J O O A C Z I
N A H M A C E L J F I V E L
R W G P U D O W G J H A N D
U X H E A R T A R O T I P L
P M N P V I M R T K G H K O
P F S I D E R D L O F K G H
```

ACE	DRAW	KING	STUD
BET	FIVE	PAIR	SUIT
BRIDGE	FLUSH	PAPER	TABLE
CALL	FOLD	PLAY	TAROT
CASINO	GAME	POKER	TEN
CLUB	GIN	QUEEN	TURN
COLOR	HAND	RED	TWO
DEAL	HEART	RULES	UNO
DECK	HOLD	RUMMY	VEGAS
DEUCE	JOKER	SPADE	WILD

Solution on page 284

Kites

```
J R O Q J U H O B B Y A L P
T G F K T X O F S T U N T H
C A F A M I L Y H H D F H T
I R W N B C D G S E I C L O
R D N O M A I D S L A G X L
B R E E Z E N I N E S A H C
A Q G V H Y G U B F P D P Y
F T F L L N R S A U C A I N
M R X F I E O I D N X B H K
H O G R P D P L G N I R T S
B P P A I H E K Y R I H I E
V S P M O C C O D N G W C A
Q D K E N B T S L I G H T R
K A D Y I C G X F A L L C T
```

AIR
ART
BEACH
BIRDS
BOX
BREEZE
CHASE
CHINA
CLOTH
DESIGN

DIAMOND
DRAG
FABRIC
FALL
FAMILY
FIGHT
FLY
FRAME
FUN
GLIDE

HEIGHT
HIGH
HOBBY
HOLDING
KIDS
LIFT
LIGHT
NYLON
PAPER
PLAY

RUN
SHAPES
SILK
SKY
SPORT
SPRING
STRING
STUNT
TOY
WIND

Solution on page 284

Fun Fun Fun

```
G L U W I S S E N L L O R D
D A F F R I V O L I T Y S I
P R M L A U G H A B L E S V
F K M E R R I M E N T S E E
N R G N I S U M A N P S N R
Y J O C O S I T Y O M E I S
T C E L E B R A T I O N C I
I C O M I C A L Z T R I U O
V R E P A C I T N A T K A N
I N I M P I S H N E S S S K
T I U S R U P O L R I I Y N
S Y D E M O C H M C L R P A
E Y T I V I T C A E N F T R
F J J M Y A L P D R O W N P
```

ACTIVITY	DIVERSION	LARK
AMUSEMENT	DROLLNESS	LAUGHABLE
AMUSING	FESTIVITY	MERRIMENT
ANTIC	FRISKINESS	PRANK
ATHLETICS	FRIVOLITY	PURSUIT
CAPER	FROLICSOME	RECREATION
CELEBRATION	GAME	ROMP
COMEDY	IMPISHNESS	SAUCINESS
COMICAL	JOCOSITY	WORDPLAY

Solution on page 284

Clowns

```
H P U E K A M F O O L I S H
O E C A F E T I H W U S L A
B R O D E O C L O W N C A R
O F M E M M A S K S F A V L
C O I I M E R G C R U R I E
O R C P E P E A I E N Y N Q
L M A E T A T G T T N C R U
O E L R T R H H S C Y O A I
R R M S K T G A P A J S C N
S S A O E I U P A R E T I S
F W G N L E A P L A S U R N
H A I R L S L Y S H T M C R
E N C G Y D E M O C E E U O
G Y S U S P E N D E R S S H
```

CARNIVAL	FOOLISH	JESTER	RED
CHARACTERS	FRIGHTENING	LAUGHTER	RODEO CLOWN
CIRCUS	FUNNY	MAGIC	SCARY
CLOWN CAR	GAGS	MAKEUP	SLAPSTICK
COLORS	HAIR	MASKS	SUSPENDERS
COMEDY	HAPPY	PARTIES	WHITEFACE
COMICAL	HARLEQUIN	PERFORMERS	WIGS
COSTUMES	HOBO	PERSON	
EMMETT KELLY	HORNS	PIE	

Solution on page 284

Let's Play Scrabble

```
D O O W Y R A L U B A C O V
G R I D C R O S S W O R D S
N K W A R D Y L I M A F U N
I N S O L A O P P O N E N T
T O S E R S O E N I L N O D
A W O U L D T B I N G O Y I
E L R G N I G N E L L A H C
H E C K T O T A I M D I J T
C D A I C O B K M O A O U I
O G V T R A M S N E P G W O
W E C B O A R D G A M E S N
H I S O T E B A H P L A U A
L A N G U A G E C L U B S R
H R U L E S N O I T I D E Y
```

ACROSS
ALPHABET
BINGO
BLANK TILES
BOARD GAMES
BONUS
CHALLENGING
CHEATING
CLUBS
COMPETITIVE
CROSSWORDS

DICTIONARY
DOWN
DRAW
EDITIONS
FAMILY
FUN
GAME BOARD
GRID
HASBRO
KNOWLEDGE
LANGUAGE

ONLINE
OPPONENT
POINTS
RACK
RULES
SMART
VOCABULARY
WIN
WOOD
WORD GAME

Solution on page 285

It's a Picnic

```
G V M E L P O E P J Y A N B
R S F R U I T I M S C R U N
W J O U I U D N D L E I F J
Z N O T T R I L O L U E A D
O H D A I C E T A D B N R A
S O B N H L H X N P T I C T
G L K I A W T U A L A W E H
E D P K A P E C R R E X N W
W S E T U O K O O C I S U M
S L E K I D S I U U H C S H
J R L M K R A P N T P L A Y
Y K H I A C B F A M I L Y R
P S S A R G I N D I N N E R
G X I K M G Y S P R I N G H
```

ANT	DOG	GRILL	PARK
BASKET	DRINK	HAM	PEOPLE
CAR	EAT	KIDS	PLAY
CHIPS	FAMILY	LAKE	RELAX
CHURCH	FIELD	LUNCH	SPRING
CLOTH	FOOD	MUSIC	SUN
COOKOUT	FRUIT	NAPKIN	TABLE
COUPLE	FUN	NATURE	TREES
DATE	GAMES	OUTING	WATER
DINNER	GRASS	PACK	WINE

Solution on page 285

CHAPTER 11

THE PHYSICAL WORLD

The Law of Gravity

```
F O R C E I N S T E I N S M
S R A T S T C E J B O E C O
Y G P R I N C I P I A X I T
R E L A T I V I T Y M P S I
E I O S T E N A L P E E Y O
T Y M O N O R T S A T R H N
T N O T W E N C A A S I P T
A C O A L E S C E E Y M P E
M P A E U N I V E R S E M N
K I C R U R A N U S R N O E
R C B S T S N O I T A T O R
A S E D I T O F A L L I N G
D H T R A E A D N U O R G Y
T C I F I T N E I C S W A L
```

ACCELERATION
ASTRONOMY
ATTRACT
COALESCE
DARK MATTER
EARTH
EINSTEIN
ENERGY
EXPERIMENT
FALLING

FORCE
GROUND
ISAAC NEWTON
LAWS
MOON
MOTION
OBJECTS
PHYSICS
PLANETS
PRINCIPIA

RELATIVITY
ROTATION
SCIENTIFIC
SOLAR SYSTEM
STARS
THE SUN
TIDES
UNIVERSE
URANUS

Solution on page 285

Bronze

```
G M S N O P A E W V A M U T
N N T J E L T T I R B E B R
T I A E S E Y M T I A D R O
H O T W T E A M R L U A A P
I C U E N T Q O P R D L S H
R Y E L E S N H A I A C S Y
D M F R M Y A B C T C A U Z
A B I Y U B L I E O R S O M
L A I C R E M M O C P T I G
L L O O T N H S I L O P C N
O S N C S C U L P T U R E O
Y Z O A N C I E N T D D R R
E S P R I N G S T L E M P T
Z I N C E A O S K B E L L S
```

AGE	COIN	MEDAL	STATUE
ALLOY	COMMERCIAL	MELT	STEEL
ALPHA BRONZE	COPPER	METAL	STRONG
ANCIENT	CYMBALS	OLYMPICS	THIRD
ART	DURABLE	ORE	TIN
BELLS	INSTRUMENTS	POLISH	TOOL
BRASS	IRON	PRECIOUS	TROPHY
BRITTLE	JEWELRY	SCULPTURE	WEAPONS
CAST	MATERIAL	SPRINGS	ZINC

Solution on page 285

Aurora

```
S P A C E P O C S E L E T A
P S N E G Y X O N I U Q E R
A S T S S E D D O G J N A C
T D N E E C N E I C S I R S
O E E O N U Y K S D B T T G
M G E R T A H E S I R R H N
S R U N C O L L I S I O N I
R A L U E C H P M P L G B R
O H B S I R T P E L L E R A
L C I T E N G A M A I N I L
O A R O R U A Y R Y A G G O
C A N A D A N E M O N E H P
P S R A T S B E A U T Y T T
M O O N I G H T R O N W A D
```

ARCS	COLORS	MAGNETIC	POLAR
ATOMS	DAWN	MOON	RED
AURORA	DISPLAY	NIGHT	RINGS
BEAUTY	EARTH	NITROGEN	SCIENCE
BLUE	EMISSIONS	NORTH	SKY
BRIGHT	ENERGY	OXYGEN	SPACE
BRILLIANT	EQUINOX	PARTICLES	STARS
CANADA	GODDESS	PHENOMENA	SUN
CHARGED	HUES	PHOTONS	TELESCOPE
COLLISION	LIGHT	PLANETS	

Solution on page 286

Avalanche

```
S T D I P A R E G N A D N S
T R S C P E O P L E K N Y K
E I P E H A Z A R D S W C I
E G L T H C R A E S A O N I
P G A P O W E R F U L D E N
O E G N I L L A F O A D G G
W R F T D T E R R A I N R N
D O L U N D E A D L Y A E I
E L O D E E D N S S S P M V
R L W E Z O D D K D O G E O
O I I I I S N I A T N U O M
C N N R S A E U C S E R N D
K G G U L R R E I C A L G D
S L A B S Z C O L L A P S E
```

ACCIDENT	EMERGENCY	MOVING	SKIERS
ALASKA	FALLING	PEOPLE	SKIING
ALPS	FLOWING	POWDER	SLAB
BURIED	FREEZING	POWERFUL	SOUND
COLLAPSE	GLACIER	RAPID	STEEP
COLORADO	HAZARD	RESCUE	TERRAIN
DANGER	ICE	ROCK	TRIGGER
DEADLY	LANDSLIDE	ROLLING	WEATHER
DOGS	LOUD	SEARCH	
DOWN	MOUNTAINS	SIZE	

Solution on page 286

Atoms

```
E N E G O R D Y H K E E R G
L U E K P D E N S E S G N D
C N L W F H N N U U P A E E
I I E A Y M Y U B O N S U G
T T M I C R O S C O P E T R
R S E O B I T L I L M M R A
A E N Y T A M S E C E B O H
P L T E N A S E I C I U N C
M L S C G I B I H M U S S M
A A E S F A T U C C E L T A
T M J E V I T I S O P H E S
T S P L I T S I T N E I C S
E P O T O S I E V C L O U D
R E Z N O I T C A E R F M B
```

BASIC
BOMB
CHARGED
CHEMICAL
CHEMISTRY
CLOUD
COMPOUND
DENSE
ELEMENTS
FISSION
GREEK

HYDROGEN
ISOTOPE
MASS
MATTER
MICROSCOPE
MOLECULES
NEGATIVE
NEUTRONS
NUCLEUS
PARTICLE
PHYSICISTS

POSITIVE
REACTION
SCIENTIST
SMALLEST
SPLIT
SUBATOMIC
SUBSTANCE
TINY
UNIT

Solution on page 286

Tidal

```
N M Y H S A W F R U S B A Y
O O L U N A R E T A W D L M
O L I L L E V E L A E S L P
M U A T A O B N O R D T U I
O F D C A K G I C H I O P M
V R S H I P E L E I T R T A
E E E E F T I T A G W M M N
B W V I L O U S N H O P A U
B O A G O C G A S T L R R S
O P W H W N Y O N I T I I T
E M I T I R D C T D D S N P
T I B R O T A U Q E N I E A
H T P E D V D I S T A N C E
E S A H P E A R T H S G C N
```

AMPLITUDE	EBB	MOVE	SAND
BAY	EQUATOR	NAUTICAL	SEA LEVEL
BOAT	FLOW	NEAP	SPRING
COASTLINE	HEIGHT	OCEANS	STORM
CYCLES	HIGH TIDE	ORBIT	SURF
DAILY	LAKE	PHASE	TIME
DEPTH	LOW TIDE	POWERFUL	TSUNAMI
DISSIPATION	LUNAR	PULL	WASH
DISTANCE	MARINE	RED	WATER
EARTH	MOON	RISING	WAVES

Solution on page 286

Mining the Earth

```
C O A L G H S U R D L O G U
S L E N N U T V E I N S S R
D I G G I N G E P F N U H A
S E N O T S P X P F I O O N
M E I H S T E T O I A R V I
E C L T A E X R C C T E E U
T R L R L E C A R U N G L M
A U I A B L A C K L U N G Y
L O R E R O V T R T O A T T
A S D N O M A I D E M D L E
D E P O S I T O I L V F A F
T R U C K M I N E R A L S A
S A G E O L O G I C A L I S
A C C I D E N T S H A F T S
```

ACCIDENT	DIFFICULT	MINERALS	SILVER
BLACK LUNG	DIGGING	MOUNTAIN	STEEL
BLASTING	DRILLING	OIL	STONES
CART	EARTH	ORE	TRUCK
COAL	EXCAVATION	PIT	TUNNELS
COPPER	EXTRACTION	RESOURCE	URANIUM
DANGEROUS	GAS	SAFETY	VEIN
DEEP	GEOLOGICAL	SALT	
DEPOSIT	GOLD RUSH	SHAFTS	
DIAMONDS	METAL	SHOVEL	

Solution on page 287

Light

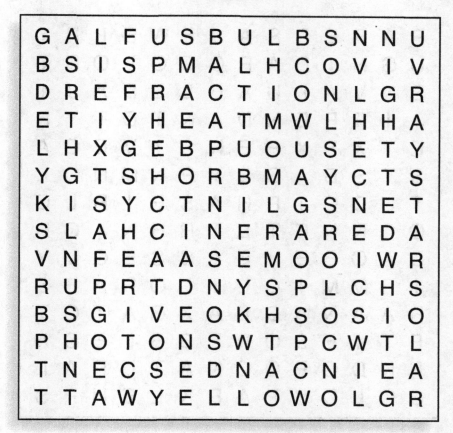

```
G A L F U S B U L B S N N U
B S I S P M A L H C O V I V
D R E F R A C T I O N L G R
E T I Y H E A T M W L H H A
L H X G E B P U O U S E T Y
Y G T S H O R B M A Y C T S
K I S Y C T N I L G S N E T
S L A H C I N F R A R E D A
V N F E A A S E M O O I W R
R U P R T D N Y S P L C H S
B S G I V E O K H S O S I O
P H O T O N S W T P C W T L
T N E C S E D N A C N I E A
T T A W Y E L L O W O L G R
```

BEAMS	GLOW	OPTICS	SHADOW
BRIGHTNESS	HEAT	PHOTONS	SKY
BULBS	ILLUMINATION	PHYSICS	SOLAR
COLORS	INCANDESCENT	POWER	SPECTRUM
ENERGY	INFRARED	RAINBOW	STARS
EYES	LAMPS	RAYS	SUNLIGHT
FAST	LED	REFRACTION	WATT
FIRE	MOON	SCIENCE	WHITE
FLASH	NIGHT	SEE	YELLOW

Solution on page 287

Gemstone

```
R A R E P S A J E W E L R Y
U G N I D A R G C O L O R T
B N V A L U A B L E D A J I
I I P P E N D A N T D T Y R
E T X E X P E N S I V E G A
S T S B A G S Y P N M N O L
T U D C I R H A S E I R L C
O C N N E T L T R H N A O R
D A O B E M E A S S E G M Y
I R M M I C L I L O R A E S
R A A N A D L A X G A T G T
E T I F S O P E B B L E S A
P N D O P O C N A T U R A L
G O L D S P A R K L E H P S
```

AGATE	DIAMONDS	JADE	PEBBLES
AMBER	EMERALDS	JASPER	PENDANT
AMETHYST	EXPENSIVE	JEWELRY	PERIDOT
BIXBITE	FACETS	LAPIDARY	POLISHING
CARAT	GARNET	MINERAL	RARE
CLARITY	GEMOLOGY	MINING	RUBIES
COLOR	GOLD	NATURAL	SPARKLE
CRYSTAL	GOSHENITE	OPAL	VALUABLE
CUTTING	GRADING	PEARL	

Solution on page 287

Natural Gas

```
X N P U M P W E L L I B O G
H T R A E N E R G Y U P S M
Y A T U W C O R E T H A N E
D T P S B D A D A N G E R H
R R C O O K I N G H O M E L
A I I U W C E P R O P A N E
T R N L D E N M M U T L M U
E E E D L O R A D U F F E F
S S G S U I R U T I L I T Y
M O O O E S N P H U U G E N
E U I V H R T G Y W R Q R A
L R B E E C V R D B I A I E
L C S N F I R E Y G R I L L
P E N G I N E S S E P I P C
```

BILL	DRILLING	GRILL	OVEN
BIOGENIC	EARTH	HEAT	PIPES
BOG	ENERGY	HOME	POWER
BURN	ENGINES	HYDRATES	PROPANE
BUTANE	ETHANE	INDUSTRY	PUMP
BYPRODUCT	FIRE	LIQUID	RESERVES
CLEAN	FLAME	MARSHES	RESOURCE
COOKING	FUEL	METER	SMELL
COST	FURNACE	NATURAL	UTILITY
DANGER	GAS	ODOR	WELL

Solution on page 287

Water Resources

```
O G S R E W O P H C P E D L
I V B S Y T I C F L O O D H
M G W E T L A S E E Z C N R
H I E C I F U H T A D A S D
M D L O I P H R S N N N W Q
A C R L A V O T U L A A A L
D R T O Q O H O A N S L M L
S E A G U G R K L B O S P E
R E P Y I G E B K S U F M W
M K U R F N H N H P R F F O
Y P R P E I I T P S C Q Q N
U U A P R R N L M A E R T S
L M I W D P Y R I V E R I J
D P N V H S I F T V Y T F K
```

AQUIFER	FILTER	PLANTS	SEA
BATH	FISH	POND	SNOW
CANAL	FLOOD	POOLS	SOURCE
CITY	FRESH	POWER	SPRING
CLEAN	GROUND	PUMP	STREAM
CREEK	ICE	RAIN	SUPPLY
DAM	LAKE	RIGHTS	SWAMP
DRINK	MILL	RIVER	SWIM
DROUGHT	OCEAN	RUNOFF	TAP
ECOLOGY	PIPE	SALT	WELL

Solution on page 288

Quantum Theory

```
Z  I  Y  T  I  V  I  T  A  L  E  R  I  C
W  U  C  H  E  M  I  S  T  R  Y  P  I  W
A  N  S  E  L  P  I  C  N  I  R  P  A  L
V  C  N  C  O  U  R  S  E  O  O  V  T  A
E  E  O  N  G  U  S  Y  B  C  E  M  O  C
M  R  R  E  Y  P  D  A  S  F  H  A  M  I
E  T  T  I  A  U  B  O  U  O  T  X  I  T
C  A  U  C  T  I  R  N  E  R  G  P  C  A
H  I  E  S  L  C  C  M  L  M  N  L  S  M
A  N  N  I  I  T  I  M  C  U  I  A  C  E
N  T  T  M  I  T  K  Z  U  L  R  N  A  H
I  Y  B  O  H  R  F  S  N  A  T  C  L  T
C  U  N  O  I  T  A  U  Q  E  S  K  E  A
S  Y  A  R  E  D  O  H  T  A  C  I  G  M
```

ATOMIC SCALE	MAX PLANCK	STRING THEORY
BOHR	NEUTRONS	STUDY
CATHODE RAYS	NUCLEUS	SUBMICROSCOPIC
CHEMISTRY	PRINCIPLES	TIME
COURSE	PROBABILITY	UNCERTAINTY
EQUATION	RELATIVITY	WAVE FUNCTION
FORMULA	SCIENCE	WAVE MECHANICS
MATHEMATICAL	SPACE	

Solution on page 288

Optics

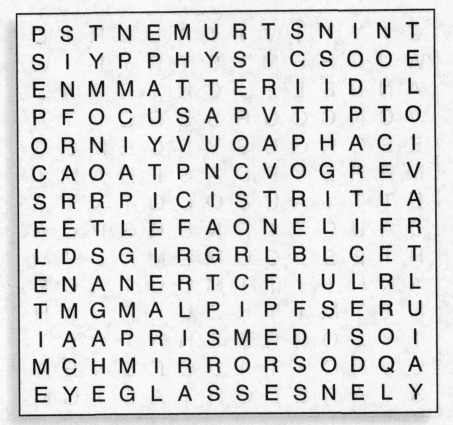

```
P S T N E M U R T S N I N T
S I Y P P H Y S I C S O O E
E N M M A T T E R I I D I L
P F O C U S A P V T T P T O
O R N I Y V U O A P H A C I
C A O A T P N C V O G R E V
S R R P I C I S T R I T L A
E E T L E F A O N E L I F R
L D S G I R G R L B L C E T
E N A N E R T C F I U L R L
T M G M A L P I P F S E R U
I A A P R I S M E D I S O I
M C H M I R R O R S O D Q A
E Y E G L A S S E S N E L Y
```

ASTRONOMY
CAMERA
DIFFRACTION
EYEGLASSES
FIBER OPTICS
FOCUS
ILLUSION
IMAGE
INFRARED

INSTRUMENTS
LENSES
LIGHT
MAGNIFICATION
MATTER
MICROSCOPES
MIRRORS
PARTICLES
PHOTOGRAPHY

PHYSICS
PRISM
PROPERTIES
PUPIL
RAYS
REFLECTION
TELESCOPES
ULTRAVIOLET

Solution on page 288

Floods

```
N I A L P I P E S R I S K M
R D A M R C U R R E N T R R
X O U F L O W A V E M F U G
W P A S T N F N B E F O G T
L A N D U T B M R O T S H Y
R M T I Y R A I N O A I Y S
T D U E I O G U E Z C T D C
C I Z D R L R E S C U E H E
O K G S R M V T A T L C A P
A E L A K E A M S T A R Y N
S S A O L N V E A E K E A O
T A E R H T A I R I D E P A
A E Y I B Y P B R T S K W H
L U W E F R G F L A S H C M
```

ARK	DELTA	NOAH	RUNOFF
BANKS	DESTROY	OCEAN	SEA
BOAT	DIKES	PIPES	STORM
BREACH	FLASH	PLAIN	STREAM
BRIDGES	FLOW	PUMP	SURGE
COASTAL	HOMES	RAIN	THREAT
CONTROL	LAKE	RESCUE	TIDE
CREEK	LAND	RISK	WATER
CURRENT	LEVEE	RIVER	WAVE
DAM	MUD	ROAD	WET

Solution on page 288

Like Wildfire

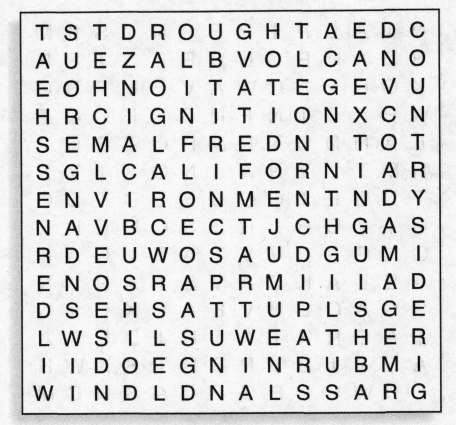

```
T S T D R O U G H T A E D C
A U E Z A L B V O L C A N O
E O H N O I T A T E G E V U
H R C I G N I T I O N X C N
S E M A L F R E D N I T O T
S G L C A L I F O R N I A R
E N V I R O N M E N T N D Y
N A V B C E C T J C H G A S
R D E U W O S A U D G U M I
E N O S R A P R M I I I A D
D S E H S A T T U P L S G E
L W S I L S U W E A T H E R
I I D O E G N I N R U B M I
W I N D L D N A L S S A R G
```

ARSON	DESTRUCTION	LIGHTNING
ASHES	DISASTER	LOSS
BLAZE	DROUGHT	NEWS
BURNING	ENVIRONMENT	RAPID
BUSH	EXTINGUISH	RED
CALIFORNIA	FLAMES	TINDER
CAMP	GRASSLAND	VEGETATION
COUNTRYSIDE	HEAT	VOLCANO
DAMAGE	HELICOPTERS	WEATHER
DANGEROUS	HILL	WILDERNESS
DEATH	IGNITION	WIND

Solution on page 289

CHAPTER 12

SPORT

Fencing

```
E J H T H R U S T I N G E G
Y G N I N O E G D U L B P R
S A N P L C I A E O A K E I
P B L U R T N L V W C S E P
A E A P L O B E R K I P E G
D C I Y D U T U L R R L U N
R N A L O R S E A O O A R I
O A A D O N O P C W T S O B
O V U P E A E W I T S T P B
N D S M J M T T S O I R E A
S A B R E E I T S O H O A T
D U E L I N G C A F M N N S
G G N I T T U C L C L I O F
W C O L Y M P I C S K S A M
```

ACADEMIC	EUROPEAN	PARISER
ADVANCE	FOIL	PLASTRON
ALDO NADI	FOOTWORK	PROTECTION
ATTACK	GLOVE	SABRE
BAYONETS	GRIP	SPADROON
BLUDGEONING	HILT	SPORT
CLASSICAL	HISTORICAL	STABBING
CUTTING	LUNGE	SWORDPLAY
DOUBLE	MASK	THRUSTING
DUELING	MENSUR	TOURNAMENT
EPEE	OLYMPICS	

Solution on page 289

Jockey

```
F F P J D L O R T N O C V S
M O U N T T M S A O W N E R
F M E N H Y A D T I O V F H
N G Y C G F B I H S V N R O
W H B A I V I G L S K M K R
E Z R R E T B R E E C H E S
I L E E H A N O T F V S N E
G Z D E T H G E E O D O T C
H J S R O L O C R R I H U A
T Z O A U E G O A P G N C R
F P W S D H B W H I P I K S
S I S I O D A E L A M A Y X
N H R L N L L B T T C R O P
G W F K S N I E R J Q T U K
```

APPRENTICE	FAST	PROFESSION
ATHLETE	HAT	RACE
AWARDS	HEIGHT	REINS
BET	HORSE	RIDE
BIB	HURDLE	SADDLE
BREECHES	KENTUCKY	SILK
CAREER	LIGHT	SPORT
COLORS	MALE	TRAIN
CONTROL	MEN	WEIGHT
CROP	MOUNT	WHIP
DERBY	OWNER	WIN

Solution on page 289

Snowboard

```
S L U S H C U P B O O T S D
H K H E A B I G A I R P G R
A A A E L L I H N W O D N Y
U J T T L Y P N J I W V I S
N F U U E M T I D I G T D L
W S R M F B E S N I B D N O
H G N E P R O T E E N V E P
I N S I E S E A S E Q G C E
T I B O A R D E R C R O S S
E V S G S T I E C D K F E E
W R E T Z X N D R A I D D M
R A I L J A M U E H R N V A
R C D R A O B W O N S V G G
K E P I P F L A H M F K E X
```

ALPINE	FREECARVE	RAIL JAM
BIG AIR	FREERIDE	SHAUN WHITE
BINDINGS	FREESTYLE	SHRED
BOARDERCROSS	GEAR	SKATEBOARDING
BOOTS	HALFPIPE	SLUSH CUP
CARVING	HELMETS	SNOWBOARD
DESCENDING	JIB	TURNS
DOWNHILL	JUMPS	UTAH
DRY SLOPES	MOUNTAINS	WINTERSTICK
EDGING	RACE	X GAMES

Solution on page 289

Squash

```
H B R E B B U R F A S T J Y
I S C R O O D N I G N I W S
T V C T R U O C C I S N Y I
R P D O E N C O O S E R V E
O Y L H R C I P M Y L O Y M
P Q E A S E O L N R G D F A
S O G L Y I E M B E N O I G
G C P L L A L T P F I U L Q
N M L U G O G G L E S B F H
I A A U L V V X N R T L O B
R F E T O A T H L E T E N W
T E U Q C A R U L E S S P Y
S J B N S H O E S P E E D R
L L A W C L U B A L L I K H
```

ATHLETE	GAME	OLYMPIC	SERVE
BALL	GOGGLES	PLAY	SHOES
BOUNCE	HIT	POINT	SINGLES
CLUB	INDOOR	POPULAR	SPEED
COMPETE	IOC	RACQUET	SPORT
COURT	KILL	RALLY	STRINGS
DOUBLES	LEAGUE	REFEREE	SWING
ENGLISH	LOB	RUBBER	TIN
FAST	MATCH	RULES	VOLLEY
FUN	NET	SCORE	WALL

Solution on page 290

Stock Car Racing

```
B O D I R T L A H P S A P E
T R O P H Y P E N U F I A W
Y E A T R S L Y R O T C A F
S P W K N M F T A C T I C S
V U S A E I Q C H E V Y R H
O S F T L S R P O P U L A R
U S S A R H S P E E D A S D
V A U E V E N T S A W P H R
F Q Y M R C E R I T T S K I
L A U T O I R T R O P S U V
A E T F T D E O E N G I N E
V C E G O E R S W I N N E R
O A A H M R P A I D E M O T
H R M R W L D C G U K L P I
```

ASPHALT	DRIVER	MEDIA	SPORT
AUTO	ENGINE	MOTOR	SPRINT
BRAKES	EVENT	OVAL	STREET
CAR	FACTORY	PETTY	SUPER
CHEVY	FANS	PIT	TACTICS
CRASH	FAST	POPULAR	TEAM
CROWD	FORD	QUALIFY	TIRE
DAYTONA	FUN	RACE	TROPHY
DIRT	HELMETS	SERIES	WHEEL
DRAG	LAPS	SPEED	WINNER

Solution on page 290

Table Tennis

```
T E A M S V A P P O I N T S
S T E N P I L F Y E L L O V
A T O H S P O R D H S U P O
F H S A M S C O I N T O S S
R E T U R N D L O H N E P U
K L S C I P M Y L O Y E I D
C O E H P L O J U L D D N D
O O L O P A D D L E S A G N
L P G P A Y A A L F H L O A
B A N N E E R G E K T B S L
G R I P R R R A C K E T S G
Y H S O J S B A C K S P I N
C Y C R E B B U R E G A M E
T S E R V E L B A T S T A B
```

ASIA	DROP SHOT	OLYMPICS	RUBBER
BACKHAND	ENGLAND	OUT	SCORE
BACKSPIN	FAST	PADDLES	SERVE
BATS	FLIP	PENHOLD	SINGLES
BLADE	GAME	PLAYERS	SMASH
BLOCK	GOSSIMA	POINTS	TABLE
CELLULOID	GREEN	PUSH	TEAMS
CHINA	GRIP	RACKETS	THE LOOP
CHOP	ITTF	RALLY	TOPSPIN
COIN TOSS	NET	RETURN	VOLLEY

Solution on page 290

Synchronized Swimming

```
F I N A P O S I T I O N S S
L I N O I T I T E P M O C M
E E G M E N D U R A N C E A
X T L U U R E T A E B G G E
I A R O R S F T H R O W S T
B R S I O E I M O V E S L U
I O T R O P S C I P M Y L O
L B E V L S H K D P L O U Y
I A U L I F T S A A K R C A
T L D B G R A C E T N H S L
Y E Y R T S I T R A I C O K
Y G E L T E L L A B G N E C
L A C I N H C E T N H Y G A
U F L A M I N G O P T S V B
```

ARTISTRY	FINA	POSITIONS
BACK LAYOUT	FLAMINGO	SCULLS
BALLET LEG	FLEXIBILITY	SIDE FISHTAIL
COMPETITION	GRACE	SYNCHRO
DANCE	KNIGHT	TEAMS
DUETS	LIFTS	TECHNICAL
EGGBEATER	MOVES	THROWS
ELABORATE	MUSIC	TRIOS
ENDURANCE	OLYMPIC SPORT	
FIGURE SKATING	POOL	

Solution on page 290

Miniature Golf

```
F F L O G S H O T N T W T R
Y E D P S E L U R O H R R A
P L A Y E R E L U I O O R M
E T I A V S E R I P L L O P
R L D M R F N M S M E L O H
O E T U A A S O E A D I D F
C L O S M F S U Y H B N N U
S C D E A L W T M C T G I N
M A N M S C I D N M I N I W
A T U E D V N O N E E R G O
L S O N I Y G O C L V R P L
L B R T K S T R O K E E L C
F O C E E D I S T U O A N F
G A M E T T U P A R B U L C
```

ACTIVITY	FELT	OUTDOORS	SHOT
AMUSEMENT	FUN	OUTSIDE	SMALL
BALL	GAME	PAR	SPORT
CASTLE	GOLF	PLAYER	STROKE
CHAMPION	GREEN	PUTT	SUMMER
CLOWN	HOLE	RAMP	SWING
CLUB	INDOOR	ROLLING	TEE
COURSE	KIDS	ROUND	THEME
EVENT	MINI	RULES	TOURNAMENT
FAMILY	OBSTACLE	SCORE	WINDMILL

Solution on page 291

Wrestling

```
S T R E N G T H S W O R H T
C N N C O U N T H C A E B P
I O A N U T R I T I O N A I
P I M O V E S A H H Q P C N
M T O P N G E N W C G O K N
Y C R U E A U I P H N S H I
L A O S L T Q M H O I I O N
O U C H Y N I A Y K K T L G
S G E I T A N T S E C I D C
N R R N S V H S I H O O I O
E E G G E D C K C O L N N A
H E N N E A E I A L N S G C
T C I E R A T L L D X Z A H
A E R M F F O L K S T Y L E
```

ACTION	FREESTYLE	POSITIONS
ADVANTAGE	GRECO ROMAN	PUSHING
ATHENS	GREECE	RAW
BACK HOLD	HOLDING	RING
BEACH	LOCKING	SKILL
CHOKE HOLDS	MEN	STAMINA
CLINCHING	MOVES	STRENGTH
COACH	NUTRITION	STRENUOUS
COMPETITION	OLYMPICS	TECHNIQUES
COUNT	PHYSICAL	THROWS
FOLK STYLE	PINNING	

Solution on page 291

Dodgeball

```
C P M U J K V S H U Y X G B
W H U R L T Y Y A L P C P S
A Y T E L C R I C L O M S E
L S N O I T A I R A V P T D
L I N E E T T V C B O A R A
K C G S E X N H O R N T O V
I A A A T Z E S T I V S H E
D L M E S N M R M S D E S D
S S E C E R E I C S I U K I
T C O C O E L D D I M G C S
O R H F M E E P U M S A U W
E U I O A I M Y G T T E D L
F N T D O D G E N C S L P Z
U O N U F L E T H R O W E U
```

AIM	EVADE	LEAGUES	SCORE
AVOID	EXERCISE	LINE	SHORTS
BALL	FOAM	MIDDLE	SIDE
CATCH	FUN	MISS	SPORT
CIRCLE	GAME	OUT	STUDENTS
COACH	GYM	PHYSICAL	TEAM
DODGE	HIT	PLAY	THROW
DUCK	HURL	RECESS	UNIFORMS
ELEMENTARY	JUMP	RUN	VARIATIONS
ELIMINATE	KIDS	SCHOOL	WALL

Solution on page 291

Croquet

```
L U T E U Q O R C F L O G M
E A T E U Q O R C O D N O M
E S B E M I T S A P I S C M
P C S T R I K E R K S S O A
E A H S U R B M N A V K B L
L T B A C K W A R D B A L L
P T P Z D S B G U Z L E P E
U E E H P E T F I L C R P T
T R G O L A F O I I K B O S
X S O B L A W N T E N N I S
E H U P U S H E N G L A N D
S O T P G A T E B A L L T Q
D T R U N S E U Q S I B S V
X M D D W C F Q L E A V E V
```

BACKWARD BALL	HOOPS	QUEEN OF GAMES
BALL IN HAND	LAWN TENNIS	RUNS
BAULK	LEAVE	RUSH
BISQUE	LIFT	SCATTER SHOT
BREAKS	MALLETS	SEXTUPLE PEEL
DOUBLE BANKING	MONDO CROQUET	STRIKER
ENGLAND	PASTIME	TICE
GATEBALL	PEG OUT	WCF
GOLF CROQUET	POINTS	
GRASS	PUSH	

Solution on page 291

Beach Volleyball

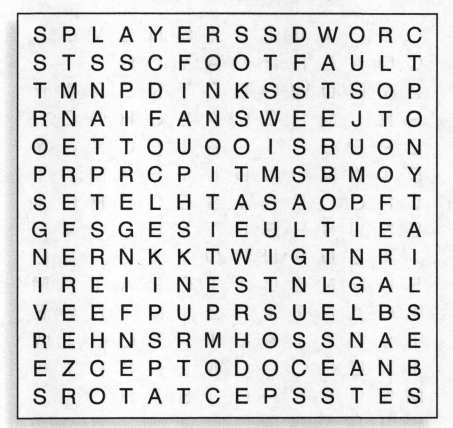

```
S P L A Y E R S S D W O R C
S T S S C F O O T F A U L T
T M N P D I N K S S T S O P
R N A I F A N S W E E J T O
O E T T O U O O I S R U O N
P R P R C P I T M S B M O Y
S E T E L H T A S A O P F T
G F S G E S I E U L T I E A
N E R N K K T W I G T N R I
I R E I I N E S T N L G A L
V E E F P U P R S U E L B S
R E H N S R M H O S S N A E
E Z C E P T O D O C E A N B
S R O T A T C E P S S T E S
```

ATHLETES	MATCH	SETS
BALL	NET	SHOT
BAREFOOT	OCEAN	SPECTATORS
CHEERS	PLAYERS	SPIKE
COMPETITION	POINTS	SPORT
CROWDS	PONYTAILS	SUNGLASSES
DINKS	POSTS	SWEAT
FANS	REFEREE	SWIMSUITS
FINGERTIPS	SANTA MONICA	TANS
FOOT FAULT	SCOREKEEPER	TRUNKS
JUMPING	SERVING	WATER BOTTLES

Solution on page 292

Little League Baseball

```
C D D I V I S I O N S Y O B
C O A C H P L A Y E R S I S
Z Y M D W O R C T N E R A P
S R L M S C C A S C H O O L
Z P E D U T S R I F C S G X
D I A M O N D L T E A M L T
L N G C P R I S C Q E R O I
E N U S R E E T N U L O V H
I I E D A H R O Y I B F E O
F N M N C C I T G P A I H M
T G A E T T P Z I M T N C E
T S G I I A M I R E O U T W
I N U R C C U W L N S D I K
M N U F E R O C S T R O P S
```

BAT	DIAMOND	GLOVE	PLAYERS
BLEACHERS	DIVISIONS	HIT	PRACTICE
BOYS	EQUIPMENT	HOME	RUN
CAPS	ESPN	INNINGS	SCHOOL
CARL STOTZ	FIELD	KIDS	SCORE
CATCHER	FIRST	LEAGUE	SPORTS
COACH	FRIENDS	MITT	TEAM
COMMUNITY	FUN	OUT	UMPIRE
CROWD	GAME	PARENT	UNIFORMS
DADS	GIRLS	PITCH	VOLUNTEERS

Solution on page 292

Basketball Madness

```
N C A A I N O I S I V I D N
V O B A S K E T B A L L F C
O L T D U K E O U C S T M O
H L N U S K B A B H N A E N
I E G U C K R I B A O R T F
O G O A N I G S L M I H S E
S E R I Z D T L E P G E Y R
T B G O A E E C T I E E S E
A H N N S R S S E O R L D N
T A C P E P U E A N A S O C
E E U D R C T J M S N K P E
G E N I L I C B S A N O B S
F I N A L F O U R C G A C P
C G N E D O O W N H O J K N
```

ARIZONA	CONFERENCE	NCAA
BASKETBALL	CONNECTICUT	OHIO STATE
BIG DANCE	DIVISION I	POD SYSTEM
BOB KNIGHT	DUKE	REGIONS
BRACKETS	ELITE EIGHT	SPRING
BUBBLE TEAMS	ESPN	TAR HEELS
CBS	FINAL FOUR	UCLA
CHAMPIONS	GAMES	UNLV
CINDERELLA	JOHN WOODEN	UPSETS
COLLEGE	KANSAS	

Solution on page 292

Fishing

```
B E S N E C I L S F G E A R
O L S I N K E R L N L K C P
W U P O D B E Y I O F O S L
F R O O O H F H P L M E C E
I E R A S I S N I P K S O A
S S T I S I T E E A C T N S
H T F H F F S T L S A H T U
I U I S N O I T A L U G E R
N N S T B T Y I V E G I S E
G A H A I S B N I V H E T E
B M I O B E B G V I T W S L
G T N L A N O W R W A T E R
S S G F N I H Q U S K O O H
K A Y A K L E I S U R E O J
```

BAITS	FLIES	LICENSE	SINKER
BANK	FLOATS	LINES	SPORT FISHING
BASS FISHING	FLY FISHING	LURES	SURVIVAL
BOAT	GEAR	NETTING	SWIVELS
BOWFISHING	HOBBYISTS	PLEASURE	TUNA
CAUGHT	HOOKS	POLE	WATER
COMPETITIONS	KAYAK	REEL	WEIGHTS
CONTESTS	LAKES	REGULATIONS	
FISHERS	LEISURE	ROD	

Solution on page 292

CHAPTER 13

ALL KINDS OF THINGS

Things for Him

```
S R E P P I L S W E B O R O
R A Z O R E Z I N A G R O M
E R T E L E V I S I O N E E
T R S Y O T E K C A J M S N
U G E T S T E G D A G O E G
P O W E R T O O L S C V N O
M L Y W B I I K T K A I C L
O F W A T C H E S H H E A O
C C L L T A K S S T W S R C
L L E L E C T R O N I C S I
L U E E I A E L G L O V E S
I B S T H T C R B O O T S U
R S C U F F L I N K S P E M
G P R A E W R E D N U D J R
```

AFTERSHAVE	GADGETS	RAZOR
BASKETBALL	GLOVES	ROBE
BEER	GOLF CLUBS	SLIPPERS
BELT	GRILL	SOCKS
BOOTS	HATS	TELEVISION
CARS	JACKET	TICKETS
CLOTHING	MOVIES	TIES
COLOGNE	MUSIC	TOYS
COMPUTERS	ORGANIZER	UNDERWEAR
CUFF LINKS	POLO SHIRTS	WALLET
ELECTRONICS	POWER TOOLS	WATCHES

Solution on page 293

Little Things

```
S G M Y M I C E C I R T M P
J B G N A T E T L F P I N S
W S R B A E L D O L T Q N A
L T A D U A L J S E U X G G
C B I I S G R B N A S S Y A
Y O N M A S M S R D D P T K
Q Z F E I U T K N A P O S Y
P N X R R C O A E U M G U C
H E Q C E D O B P S N E D I
F T A S T C L I P L E R E A
W T N L C F K I N S E M E A
N I R I A H D L H S D S S O
J K W A B E F S E C L I P J
M K L N R U M O U S E B K L
```

ANT	DIME	KIDS	PUPPY
ATOM	DNA	KITTEN	QUARK
BABY	DUST	MARBLE	RICE
BACTERIA	FLEA	MICE	RING
BEADS	FRECKLE	MITE	SALT
BUG	GERMS	MOUSE	SEED
CELL	GNAT	NAILS	SPIDER
CHILDREN	GRAIN	NEEDLE	STAPLES
COINS	HAIR	PEA	TOES
CRUMBS	INSECTS	PINS	

Solution on page 293

Things for Kids

```
U S E O H S O C K S J Z D Y
S L E G O C H E C K E R S D
L E I I B I C Y C L E R I N
L D B P U Z Z L E S A N S A
O S R E T O O C S C O B K C
D R A O B E T A K S T A C T
M E B O A R D G A M E B O Y
O L S Y O T R U C K S Y L G
V C D N D C R A Y O N S B L
I Y I O W S R E K C I T S O
E C P P S N O O L L A B N V
S I B E A R S E L B R A M E
S R E K R A M C L O T H E S
S T E R E O I D A R E K I B
```

BABY	CHECKERS	LEGO	SLEDS
BALLOONS	CLOTHES	MARBLES	SOCKS
BARBIE	CRAYONS	MARKERS	STEREO
BEARS	DINOSAUR	MOVIES	STICKERS
BICYCLE	DOLLS	PONY	TOYS
BIKE	DRESS	PUZZLES	TRAIN SET
BLOCKS	ELECTRONICS	RADIO	TRICYCLE
BOARD GAME	GAMEBOY	SCOOTER	TRUCKS
CANDY	GLOVES	SHOES	
CARS	IPOD	SKATEBOARD	

Solution on page 293

Things That Crawl

```
Y B A B G W W R O A C H E S
E A E U P Q O C I F F A R T
K E L I T P E R E I B A R C
N S T L S E T I M R E T R E
O T R A I K D C I H T O L S
M N U I L G I E T I C K S N
C A T S V C A N P O H P C I
S O K C E G R T D I I D O S
L I Z A R D S I O P L J R W
I G Z C F P L P C R D L P I
A U U L I E I E I K E C I M
N B E D S T O D D L E R O M
S A E B H B E E T L E T N E
S R A T S L O B S T E R S R
```

ALLIGATOR	CROCODILE	RATS	SWIMMER
ANT	CUBS	REPTILE	TERMITES
BABY	FLEAS	ROACHES	TICKS
BEETLE	GECKOS	SCORPION	TIME
BUG	INSECTS	SILVERFISH	TODDLER
CATS	LIZARD	SKIN	TRAFFIC
CENTIPEDE	LOBSTERS	SLOTH	TURTLE
CHILD	MICE	SLUG	WORM
CRAB	MILLIPEDE	SNAIL	
CRICKETS	MONKEY	SPIDER	

Solution on page 293

Red Things

```
H S I D A R A S H E S J L V
M T Z I O N R P R S K C O S
E N H Z B O B E P E S L B N
A A C G R O L A D L P I S G
T R N B I L B B R H E P T I
Q D U E C L O W N N O S E S
K Y P R K A C R L O D T R P
G H T R A B B I T E Y E S O
C E I Y B U R A F H E A R T
W S U N S E T H Z F C A R S
A O R S A N T A C L A U S C
G R F I L I H C H E R R Y P
O T A M O T H G I L P O T S
N S S E R D S E O H S I N K
```

APPLE	CRAYON	MEAT	SOCKS
BALLOON	DRESS	PEPPER	STOP SIGN
BARN	DYE	RABBIT EYES	STOPLIGHT
BERRY	FRUIT PUNCH	RADISH	SUNSET
BLOOD	HAIR	RASHES	TOMATO
BRICK	HEART	RED HOTS	TRAFFIC LIGHT
CAR	HYDRANTS	ROSE	WAGON
CHERRY	INK	RUBY	
CHILI	LIPS	SANTA CLAUS	
CLOWN NOSES	LOBSTER	SHOES	

Solution on page 294

Big Things

```
S K Y W V E Y X A L A G Y S
K H N D I N O S A U R O E U
R O I S U P L A N E T C L B
A U A U E N T N A H P E L E
H S T N E N I T N O C A A A
S E N A R C W V M T L N V R
H L U P T A R R E D L U O B
T A O Q L E F F A R I G R B
R H M L D U S N O I S N A M
E W O W G H G G R E B E C I
S T O A I I O G E K C U R T
E O N P Y R A M I D E A T E
D S T A R H I N O B C R P J
H L D J S A X E T O W E R S
```

BEAR	ELEPHANT	MOON	SPACE
BIG GULP	GALAXY	MOUNTAIN	STAR
BOULDER	GIANT	OCEAN	SUN
BUS	GIRAFFE	PLANET	TEXAS
CAR	GREAT WALL	PYRAMID	TOWER
CONTINENT	HOUSE	REDWOOD	TREE
CRANE	ICEBERG	RHINO	TRUCK
DESERT	IDEA	SHARKS	UNIVERSE
DINOSAUR	JET	SHIP	VALLEY
EGO	MANSION	SKY	WHALE

Solution on page 294

Morning Things

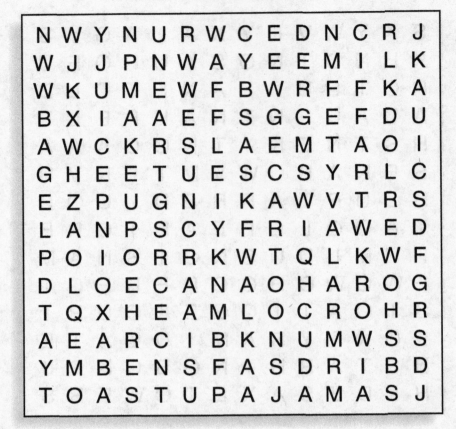

```
N W Y N U R W C E D N C R J
W J J P N W A Y E E M I L K
W K U M E W F B W R F F K A
B X I A A E F S G G E F D U
A W C K R S L A E M T A O I
G H E E T U E S C S Y R L C
E Z P U G N I K A W V T R S
L A N P S C Y F R I A W E D
P O I O R R K W T Q L K W F
D L O E C A N A O H A R O G
T Q X H E A M L O C R O H R
A E A R C I B K N U M W S S
Y M B E N S F A S D R I B D
T O A S T U P A J A M A S J
```

ALARM	DAY	OATMEAL	TOAST
AWAKE	DEW	PAJAMAS	TRAFFIC
BACON	DONUTS	PANCAKES	VITAMINS
BAGEL	EGGS	PAPER	WAFFLE
BED	EXERCISE	RUN	WAKING UP
BIRDS	HAM	SCHOOL	WALK
BREAKFAST	JUICE	SHOWER	WORK
CARTOONS	MAKEUP	SLEEPY	YAWN
CEREAL	MILK	SUN	
COFFEE	NEWS	TEA	

Solution on page 294

Yellow Things

```
K C I H C T C H E E S E R P
F R Q E G D O N O M E L L E
L A H C R A E E I T G E T N
V Y D I A I E L D R A W O C
I O A D P S E P F F P X S I
H N O N E Y B P L L W P I L
S O R U F R D A F F O D I L
A I K A R A G S U N L W M M
U L C J U I T F G C L N E A
Q E I F I N P E P P E R S R
S D R I T C B E G G Y O L K
T N B S N O O L L A B C C E
A A J H B A N A N A B U S R
R D R I B T N I A P D Y P E
```

APPLE	CORN	FLOWER	RAINCOAT
BALLOONS	COWARD	GRAPEFRUIT	SMILEY FACES
BANANA	CRAYON	JAUNDICE	SPONGEBOB
BEE	DAFFODIL	LEAF	SQUASH
BIRD	DAISY	LEMON	STAR
BRICK ROAD	DANDELION	MARKER	SUN
BUS	DUCK	PAINT	TAXI
CHEESE	EGG YOLK	PENCIL	YELLOW PAGES
CHICK	FISH	PEPPERS	

Solution on page 294

Things for Her

```
P S K I R T T E L E C A R B
E S C I N O R T C E L E A P
R R P H T S G N I R R A E M
F E W A T C H T S D S F W C
U P E P V E H C R E U R R A
M P X A E I I E V R O E E S
E I P J A T S R N S S Y D H
C L E A E S A I E W S R N M
A S N M K C T L T G A D U E
L B S A S U D O O C N R C R
K O I S R N W L T C O I E E
C O V E A E D F R F O A L P
E K E C L D I S H E S H T H
N S Z S G G N I H T O L C S
```

BOOKS	DRESS	NECKLACE
BRACELET	EARRINGS	PAJAMAS
CANDLES	ELECTRONICS	PERFUME
CASHMERE	EXPENSIVE	SCARVES
CDS	FURNITURE	SKIRT
CHOCOLATE	GIFT CARDS	SLIPPERS
CLOTHING	GOLD	SPA VISIT
COATS	HAIR DRYER	TOWELS
COSMETICS	KITCHENWARE	UNDERWEAR
DISHES	LINGERIE	WATCH

Solution on page 295

Black Things

```
C T R T O O S P A C E F D T
T E S A F T A B U U R I H K
W V K R N O R I E P R G Y B
N C T A H P N U P T I A U Y
R Y I B U K J Y L N D L E Y
G C E L O H X B X I L Z S B
H R E Y N O Y A R C O T E O
X O A G E D T F J U E C L A
O W B V R R X S G K I I T P
S E N E E F F O C G V S E C
E P S D L N D A A E U P E G
O S I R X T J M S T P C B S
H P L A O C S U H E A R T C
S W I T C H R U R R F Z U C
```

ANTS	COFFEE	HOLE	PEPPER
BAT	CRAYON	HORSE	PUPILS
BEAR	CROW	INK	RAVEN
BEETLES	DIRT	IRON	SHOES
BELTS	DOG	JACKETS	SOOT
BOOTS	DRESS	MAGIC	SPACE
BRUISES	EYE	NIGHT	SPIDER
BULL	FRIDAY	OIL	TAR
CAR	HAT	OLIVES	TIE
COAL	HEART	ONYX	WITCH

Solution on page 295

Things on Wheels

```
K D U D L D Y O F E F R T L
C A P S P W E D Y E O I V M
U U E T E H L K E L U X L O
R T E A A E L R L C R A U W
T O J G I E O E C Y W T G E
N M M E R L R L Y C H R G R
S O O C P B T C C I E I A E
E B P O L A O Y R N E C G T
T I E A A R I C O U L Y E O
A L D C N R R I T E E C C O
K E O H E O A B O T R L A C
S K L G Q W H A M S T E R S
I Z L N A V C H A I R S U B
W C Y T R A I N O G A W E B
```

AIRPLANE	JEEP	TRAIN
AUTOMOBILE	LUGGAGE	TRICYCLE
BICYCLE	MOPED	TROLLEY
BUS	MOTORCYCLE	TRUCK
CAR	MOWER	UNICYCLE
CHAIRS	ROLLERBLADES	VAN
CHARIOT	SCOOTER	WAGON
DOLLY	SKATES	WHEELBARROW
FOUR WHEELER	STAGECOACH	
HAMSTERS	TAXI	

Solution on page 295

Smooth Things

```
F T V T C L E G S R U F P Z
V M A R B L E H O I L T U Z
X E E K U D E T Q F R N D Z
U A L H T E A Y R O V I D A
M I A V T R N O R Q R A I J
S I S S E D S R V T E P N E
R T H P R T I B R H H P G L
I P O D I M A U D N T L R I
Y E S N S L G L Q Q A E O T
V A G S L O A S O I E C A F
A R A O Y B A B Y C L I D S
R L O T I O N F L O O R S K
G N I T A S A U C E L H D I
R E T A W G R N K L A T C N
```

APPLE	FUR	LIQUID	SATIN
BABY	GLASS	LOTION	SAUCE
BALD HEAD	GRAVY	MARBLE	SHEETS
BALLOON	HAIR	MIRROR	SILK
BUTTER	ICE	OIL	SKIN
CHOCOLATE	IVORY	OPERATOR	TALK
CREAM	JAZZ	PAINT	TILE
FACE	LEATHER	PEARL	VELVET
FLOORS	LEGS	PUDDING	WATER
FROSTING	LIPS	ROADS	YOGURT

Solution on page 295

Things That Are Green

```
T D W E A L T H R O L O C O
R C P A R R O T E F R O G S
E E L T R U T D S I R I S H
E K C O R M A H S E V A E L
S C H A V J E M I L R P N S
A I R E M E R A L D S O N P
E S I C R O R E M S Y A F I
P T S U Y S U O L A E J R G
A N T T P H S F R B U E E M
I A M T D S C C L S L M C E
N L A E L G N U J A O D Y N
T P S L T N I T N N G Y C T
S S A R G A R D E N B E L E
L D S K E L L Y G R E N E A
```

BEANS	FOREST	KELLY	PIGMENT
CAMOUFLAGE	FROGS	LEAVES	PLANTS
CHRISTMAS	GARDEN	LETTUCE	RECYCLE
CLOVER	GRASS	LIME	SHAMROCK
COLOR	HUE	MONEY	SICK
CRAYON	IRELAND	MOSS	TEA
DYE	IRISH	NATURE	TINT
EMERALDS	JADE	PAINT	TREES
ENERGY	JEALOUSY	PARROT	TURTLE
FIELDS	JUNGLE	PEAS	WEALTH

Solution on page 296

Hot Things

```
V L T B J K R A P S B R R T
R E S A L A V A N T Q O E R
A R S V O L C A N O Q T P K
X D B U R N E R E H R A P Q
G N I N O S A E S D V I E S
I A Z E N H C Z T E O D P A
E S Z A C X N I M R V A F U
S U U A H A Q E P Z E R I C
E N C E I L N E E O N S R E
T H A D L T D R C R R M E U
Z A J I I H S O U P G T V D
Z E R A R D E E F F O C E N
G G M A T C H L E M A L F O
Z E K T P L G D L Q D O O F
```

BURNER	FURNACE	MATCH	SOUP
CHILI	GREENHOUSE	OVEN	SPARK
COFFEE	GRILL	PAVEMENT	SUN
DESERT	HELL	PEPPER	TAR
FEVER	IDEA	RADIATOR	TEA
FIRE	IRON	RED HOTS	TROPICS
FLAME	JACUZZI	SAND	VOLCANO
FONDUE	LASER	SAUCE	
FOOD	LAVA	SEASONING	

Solution on page 296

Cold Things

```
M I L K O A B Y Q D B S T W
R T G E T E H S U L S K I J
E E E L E T S N I U G N E P
H E F R O S T Z Y I D I C G
T L C R C O Z R E V I R O S
A S S N I A T N U O M D O H
E A D S R G O C E A N E L E
W L F D E B E G L A C I E R
O A R S O D A R N I A R R B
N S I B E R I A A H P V L E
S K D O E L O P H T R O N T
M A G V S O U T H P O L E E
H R E Z E E R F M P N R D E
Z B M Q M M R I N S T X Z F
```

ALASKA	HAIL	RIVER
BEER	ICE	SHERBET
BEVERAGE	IGLOO	SIBERIA
BLIZZARD	MILK	SLEET
COOLER	MOUNTAINS	SLUSH
DRINKS	NORTH POLE	SNOW
FEET	OCEAN	SODA
FREEZER	PENGUINS	SOUTH POLE
FRIDGE	POOL	TEA
FROST	RAIN	WEATHER
GLACIER	REFRIGERATOR	WIND

Solution on page 296

CHAPTER 14

OUTSIDE

Hit the Trail

```
S P A M S R E K I H S W B N
G K E R U T N E V D A M A T
N B R U N N I N G L I T O R
I A D A R E A A K L U P A A
K C I O P E S I C R E X E V
I K R S S E N R E D L I W E
B P T E Z G I T E E E O O L
I A R S T F A S D V V S L P
C C O R G O T E I A A L L O
Y K A O N R N U U P R A O E
C I D H I E U Q G W G M F P
L N S A K S O E R O S I O N
E G N D I T M A R K I N G S
R P A T H S Y A W K L A W Y
```

ADVENTURE	FOLLOW	PARKS
ANIMALS	FOREST	PATHS
AREA	GRAVEL	PAVED
BACKPACKING	GUIDE	PEDESTRIAN
BICYCLE	HIKERS	PEOPLE
BIKING	HIKING	RUNNING
CLIMB	HORSES	TRAVEL
DIRT ROAD	MAPS	WALKING TRAIL
EQUESTRIAN	MARKINGS	WALKWAY
EROSION	MOUNTAINS	WILDERNESS
EXERCISE	NATURE	

Solution on page 296

Utility Poles

```
S D R I B M I L C Y L L A T
W E V P O W E R I T E L O P
I T N O E C I V R E S P V B
R A N I L A E O T F H O E O
E L V E P T P T C A O S R U
K U C E M P A O E S C T H T
R S R U U P A G L R K R E S
O N P S R X I S E S C O A I
W I U D I R G U T E H N D D
E L B A C Y E H Q R N G O E
D E L I N E G N J E E O I C
A E I H E I G H T O W E H H
O T C V L X E N E R G Y T P
R S C O M P A N Y R O U N D
```

ANTENNAS	EQUIPMENT	PINE	SHOCK
BIRDS	GRID	POLE	STEEL
CABLE	HEIGHT	POST	STREET
CLIMB	HIGH	POWER	STRONG
COAXIAL	INSULATED	PUBLIC	SUPPORT
COMPANY	LIGHTS	REPAIR	TALL
CONCRETE	LINE	ROAD	VOLTAGE
CURRENT	OUTSIDE	ROUND	WIRE
ELECTRIC	OVERHEAD	SAFETY	WOOD
ENERGY	PHONE	SERVICE	WORKER

Solution on page 297

Dunes

```
W G E E S A H A R A E S E B
I N M V A C I R F A W O L B
N O Q R A L I N E A R S P Y
D L S E I J R E V I R D P B
S U T C N D O D N A L N I E
T T N R R V N M O C T U R A
O A A E O T I A I C E O E C
R L L A F R A R S L E M H H
M L P T I I Y E O L I A K A
W D S I L D E H R N L A N B
A R S O A G L L E G M I R I
V Y A N C E L O D A K E H T
E K R A P L A N O I T A N A
Y E G R A L V R E T A W C T
```

AFRICA	GREAT	MOUNDS	SAND
BEACH	HABITAT	NATIONAL PARK	SCIENCE
BLOW	HEAT	OCEAN	SEA
CALIFORNIA	HILLS	OLD	STORM
DOME	HOT	PLANTS	TALL
DRY	INLAND	RECREATION	TRAIL
DUNE FIELD	LARGE	RIDGE	VALLEY
ENVIRONMENT	LINEAR	RIPPLE	WATER
EROSION	LONG	RIVER	WAVE
GRASS	MOJAVE	SAHARA	WINDS

Solution on page 297

Australia's Great Barrier Reef

```
S T N E M N O R I V N E N E
S L M A B S A L T W A T E R
D A A U O E D S C G T S D A
S N R S A L E Y A N U E I E
P D I T T T D I I R G V L
Y M N R S R C N R H A R I C
L A E A Q U E E N S L A N D
O R P L Z T T Y S I B L G O
P K A I G A O L S F E E R L
L F R A S E R I S L A N D P
A F K N P S P G A B U C S H
R E D N O W L A R U T A N I
O E C O S Y S T E M Y F U N
C L O W N F I S H A R K S S
```

AUSTRALIA	ENVIRONMENT	PROTECTED
BOATS	FISHING	QUEENSLAND
CAIRNS	FRASER ISLAND	REEFS
CLEAR	FUN	SALTWATER
CLOWNFISH	LANDMARK	SCUBA
CORAL POLYPS	LARGEST	SEA TURTLES
DIVING	MARINE PARK	SHARKS
DOLPHINS	NATURAL BEAUTY	SYDNEY
ECOSYSTEM	NATURAL WONDER	

Solution on page 297

Niagara Falls

```
T N U T S L L A F R E T A W
U L U N A I S L A N D M S E
N K R A M D N A L K E R U L
I X E G R O G N U R K E D E
T I S I V Y R A I A R V D C
E P R O S P E C T P O I N T
D S E N I M A D H D Y R A R
S P I I W N T N G B W A L I
T O C S F A L A I U E R S C
A P A A W T A L E F N A I I
T U L C E U K L H F T G T T
E L G E I R E E K A L A A Y
S A V C V E S W O L F I O F
X R C H O N E Y M O O N G B
```

AMERICAN FALLS	GREAT LAKES	POPULAR
BOAT	HEIGHT	PROSPECT POINT
BUFFALO	HONEYMOON	STUNT
CASINO	LAKE ERIE	UNITED STATES
DAM	LANDMARK	USA
ELECTRICITY	LUNA ISLAND	VIEW
FLOW	NATURE	VISIT
GLACIERS	NEW YORK	WATERFALLS
GOAT ISLAND	NIAGARA RIVER	WELLAND CANAL
GORGE	PARK	

Solution on page 297

Bird Feeders

```
E T R A Y P E R C H C T A W
S L C W I N D O W O O D C I
F O O D O D T D I U Q I L L
H L R P E R C I T S A L P D
T Z N E E I R D Z E S L M R
F H F E G B O A E M P T Y A
G I B S D O W I P U E W G Y
S Z L E R R I U Q S C N T N
V R U L R R A S V R I T U V
T A E O X U E G E G E T B Y
B T J I W E T T N L S C E N
S C A R D I N A L T A B L E
U E Y O S I H I N I B O R S
W N Y J W W M O P T S U E T
```

BIRD	GARDEN	OUTDOOR	TABLE
BLUE JAY	HANGING	PERCH	TRAY
CARDINAL	HOUSE	PLASTIC	TREE
CORN	LIQUID	POLE	TUBE
CROW	MILLET	ROBIN	WATCH
EAT	NATURE	SEED	WILD
EMPTY	NECTAR	SPARROW	WINDOW
FEED	NEST	SPECIES	WINTER
FILL	NUTS	SQUIRREL	WOOD
FOOD	ORIOLES	SUET	YARD

Solution on page 298

Ecosystem

```
D E S E R T S E R O F C T Y
T M I Y P T A T I B A H R E
U O W G H Q C M A R I N E R
N I M O Y G O L O M Y T E P
D B S L S V A L I T H W S G
R I I O I N F L I M P E E N
A R N C C S A N S S A A C I
T D A E A A U R O U R T N V
S S G A L M N N I R G H E I
T N R N M R A N L V O E I L
E F O O D W E B A I E R C I
P T C A R E T N I V G R S F
P P I C I T A U Q A A H S E
E R U T A N I M A L S S T U
```

AIR	ECOLOGY	LIFE	SAVANNA
ANIMALS	ETYMOLOGY	LIVING	SCIENCE
AQUATIC	FAUNA	MARINE	SOIL
BALANCE	FLORA	NATURE	STEPPE
BIOME	FOOD WEB	OCEAN	SUNLIGHT
BIRDS	FOREST	ORGANISM	SURVIVAL
CLIMATE	GEOGRAPHY	PHYSICAL	TREES
COMMUNITY	HABITAT	PREY	TUNDRA
DESERT	INTERACT	RIVERS	WEATHER

Solution on page 298

Intertidal

```
E A G L A N O T K N A L P L
N D Z M S U P O I R G I T M
O O S E A U R C H I N T C U
I P I A S U B S T R A T E S
S I L T N P R E D A T O R S
R H B E I D R Y S B A R C E
E P A W K T F M O T A I D L
M M L S U P E L O H C N O C
M A A E D I T P E C L A M A
I J N C H T H A M A L U S N
M G U L L S D O P O S I P R
A B S R E T A W Y K C O R A
O H E U K A R Y O T E K A B
F L I A N S A L I N I T Y C
```

ALGAE	EUKARYOTE	ROCKY
AMPHIPODA	FOAM	SALINITY
BALANUS	GULLS	SAND FLEAS
BARNACLES	IMMERSION	SEA URCHIN
CHTHAMALUS	ISOPODS	SNAIL
CLAM	KELP	SPRAY
COMPETITION	LITTORINA	SUBSTRATES
CONCHOLEPUS	MUSSEL	TIDE
CRABS	PLANKTON	TIGRIOPUS
DIATOM	PREDATORS	WATER

Solution on page 298

Fence

```
N Z Y M L L W E L O P O S T
I E E B L W H I T E D G B E
V S D A A V C O R A O K D P
H G T G W I L Y U E G N F M
Z Z U E E N O T S S F I H V
V S J A E Y S R T N E L B O
R G R P R L E E P L N O R I
J U M P O D K U D A C E I D
K S L O R C O N T A I N C O
Q T P O I I E M P R N N K O
Z V B P Q D V R R A G S T W
K C O L R S L A M I N A Y I
U N I A H C B F C L I M B O
O C G N S A F E T Y A R D H
```

ANIMALS	FARM	LOCK	SAFETY
BARRIER	FENCING	MESH	STEEL
BORDER	FIELD	PAINT	STONE
BRICK	GARDEN	PET	TALL
CHAIN	GATE	PICKET	VINYL
CLIMB	GUARD	POLE	WALL
CLOSE	HOUSE	POOLS	WHITE
CONTAIN	IRON	POST	WIRE
DOG	JUMP	PRIVACY	WOOD
EDGE	LINK	RAIL	YARD

Solution on page 298

226

Tree House

```
F  Z  S  D  S  T  I  L  T  S  D  I  K  Q
K  A  U  T  A  Y  E  T  E  B  W  W  B  U
W  N  R  O  O  D  H  C  F  O  R  T  M  I
E  T  U  T  H  O  R  O  D  L  N  G  I  S
M  S  D  R  Y  E  L  N  U  T  R  D  L  X
O  R  U  E  T  M  I  S  M  S  L  N  C  C
H  E  P  E  N  W  E  G  D  I  E  U  J  L
I  M  R  B  R  O  P  E  H  N  S  F  E  U
G  M  E  K  R  P  T  C  V  T  E  V  A  B
H  A  B  I  T  A  T  I  O  N  O  I  U  D
Y  H  M  D  V  I  N  M  S  B  W  I  R  R
A  L  U  E  U  N  A  C  A  B  L  E  S  F
R  P  L  A  Y  T  I  Z  H  D  W  X  I  L
D  E  P  P  X  F  L  W  O  O  D  V  X  V
```

ABOVE	DAD	HIGH	SECRET
ANTS	DEN	HOME	SIGN
BOLTS	DOOR	HOUSE	STILTS
BRANCH	ELEVATED	KIDS	TOOLS
BUILD	FORT	LUMBER	TREE
CABLES	FRIENDS	NAIL	TRUNK
CHILD	FUN	PAINT	VIEW
CLIMB	HABITATION	PLAY	WINDOW
CLUB	HAMMER	ROPE	WOOD
CUSTOM	HEIGHT	SAW	YARD

Solution on page 299

Mount Everest

```
H D A N G E R O U S K A E P
I S K I D S A Y A L A M I H
K S N O W E G G A S C E N T
E S N O I T A V E L E E G E
B A E X I R L T T T P H R G
A P V P M T F S H A F U E N
S R R A O V I I L Z T V A E
E E T U L R N D H N O K T L
C H H G U A W W E R D N A L
A S A O I I N V I P O L E A
M B T R S S D C G C X C O H
P E R U T A N I H C E E K C
V F R O S T B I T E B I T S
W S R E B M I L C L O U D S
```

ADVENTURE	CLOUDS	HEIGHT	SAGARMATHA
ANDREW WAUGH	COLD	HIKE	SHERPAS
ASCENT	DANGEROUS	HIMALAYAS	SKI
ASIA	DEATH ZONE	ICE	SNOW
AVALANCHE	ELEVATION	NATURE	THIN AIR
BASE CAMP	EXPEDITIONS	NEPAL	TIBET
CHALLENGE	FLAG	PEAKS	TOURIST
CHINA	FROSTBITE	ROCKS	
CLIMBERS	GREAT	ROPES	

Solution on page 299

Garden

```
M F E L K B H C L U M K A K
L R O S E S O N I A R E C W
B E T N L M S A Y B A O P S
L S C O P D D T I U R F A O
T H O O O T E U S N E E T I
X T S O P S B R E K T P H L
I T F I S A N E A I A O A N
H Q O A L D R R A B W N V T
H W R S W G E K U U D D T M
Q G M E Y I N S E C T S W O
K Z A V W A H E I D W Y H S
L F L O W E R D N G E E O G
L I R L S E E D U K N N E I
D G X G N I R P S E E R T D
```

BEAUTY	FOOD	INSECTS	ROSES
BEDS	FORMAL	LAND	SEED
BENCH	FRESH	MULCH	SOIL
BUSHES	FRUIT	NATURE	SPRING
COMPOST	GLOVES	PARK	SUN
DESIGN	GRASS	PATH	TOOLS
DIG	GREEN	PONDS	TREES
EDEN	GROW	RAIN	WATER
ENGLISH	HERB	RAKE	WEED
FLOWER	HOE	ROCK	YARD

Solution on page 299

Kelp Forest

```
G N I V I D E T C E T O R P
K T R O P I C A L J E L G A
L D V D H M O B E Y T I R C
A E I O A A S U V C A F O I
T N C O B C Y C I N R E W F
S S I F I R S S T A E A T I
A I T M T O T K C Y P H H C
O T A D A A E E U O M A C I
C Y U N T L M L D U E R R T
D D Q A P G S P O B T V A C
A L A S K A X B R K F E E R
L O B S T E R E P I T S S A
P C Q V H O L D F A S T E A
F R O N D S M S I N A G R O
```

ALASKA	FRONDS	PACIFIC
ANIMALS	GIANT KELP	PRODUCTIVE
AQUATIC	GROWTH	PROTECTED
ARCTIC	HABITAT	REEF
BUOYANCY	HARVEST	RESEARCH
COASTAL	HOLDFAST	SAND
COLD	KELP BEDS	SCUBA
DENSITY	LIFE	STIPE
DIVING	LOBSTER	TEMPERATE
ECOSYSTEM	MACROALGAE	TROPICAL
FOOD	ORGANISMS	

Solution on page 299

Around the Beach

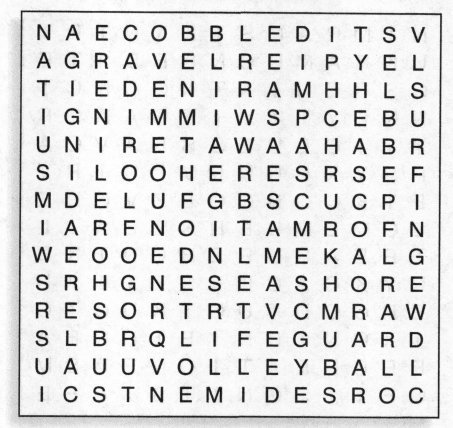

```
N A E C O B B L E D I T S V
A G R A V E L R E I P Y E L
T I E D E N I R A M H H L S
I G N I M M I W S P C E B U
U N I R E T A W A A H A B R
S I L O O H E R E S R S E F
M D E L U F G B S C U C P I
I A R F N O I T A M R O F N
W E O O E D N L M E K A L G
S R H G N E S E A S H O R E
R E S O R T R T V C M R A W
S L B R Q L I F E G U A R D
U A U U V O L L E Y B A L L
I C S T N E M I D E S R O C
```

BONDI BEACH	LAKE	SHELL
CALIFORNIA	LIFEGUARD	SHORELINE
CLAMS	MARINE	SUMMER
COBBLE	OCEAN	SURFING
CRABS	PEBBLES	SWIMMING
CURRENTS	PIER	SWIMSUIT
FLORIDA	READING	TAN
FORMATION	RECREATION	TIDE
GEOGRAPHY	RESORT	VOLLEYBALL
GRAVEL	SEASHORE	WARM
HAWAII	SEDIMENTS	WATER

Solution on page 300

Geocaching Fun

```
N I M R A G S T E K N I R T
U K R A M H C N E B D A T E
G S R E N I A T N O C N C T
N N E Y T I V I T C A A O R
I Y I C L U E S S E A V O A
R S Y X F U N P V L D I R V
E T K O O B G O L Z V G D E
E O M E M B E R S Z E A I L
T R E A S U R E H U N T N B
N Y K C A C H E S P T I A U
E R O O D T U O T K U O T G
I X G N I D N I F T R N E A
R E C R E A T I O N E A S M
O E T I S G N I T S I L F E
```

ACTIVITY	GAME	PUZZLE
ADVENTURE	GARMIN	RECREATION
BENCHMARK	GPS	SCAVENGER HUNT
CACHES	LETTERBOXING	STORY
CLUES	LISTING SITE	TRAVEL BUG
CONTAINERS	LOGBOOK	TREASURE HUNT
COORDINATES	MEMBERS	TRINKETS
DATE	NAVIGATIONAL	USE
FINDING	ORIENTEERING	
FUN	OUTDOOR	

Solution on page 300

CHAPTER 15

ENTERTAINMENT

Monty Python

```
E T I T F E R I T A S G T T
S H S O L N E K J H O N M H
K E E R Y G T S O U E I A E
L P I R I L H E H M D T I G
A Y V A N I G R N O I C L O
W T O P G S U I C R V A L O
Y H M I C H A E L P A L I N
L O P Z I T L S E S O N G S
L N A I R B F O E F I L Y P
I S J E C B B H S I T I R B
S U T F U N N Y E P U O R T
R N B M S E N O J Y R R E T
E W O H S H C T E K S P T O
D F P S R E M R O F R E P G
```

ACTING
BBC
BRITISH
ENGLISH
ENTERTAINMENT
FLYING CIRCUS
FUNNY
HUMOR
JOHN CLEESE

LAUGHTER
LIFE OF BRIAN
MICHAEL PALIN
MOVIES
PARROT
PERFORMERS
SATIRE
SERIES
SILLY WALKS

SKETCH SHOW
SONGS
TERRY GILLIAM
TERRY JONES
THE GOONS
THE PYTHONS
TROUPE
VIDEO

Solution on page 300

Country Music

```
O H I L L B I L L Y R I C S
I O F S C O N C E R T B Z S
D N N O I S I V E L E T T S
A K S L L N H B A N J O K R
R Y B T L K G O E D O R P A
S T L S R I M E W R H O T T
O O U L T U H U R S N Y E I
U N E O I S M H S S N A N U
T K G V G B I E T I Y C N G
H Q R E T K A T N I C U E E
E B A L L A D K R T A F S N
R O S Y O B W O C A S F S R
N A S H V I L L E O H N E E
S O N G S P E R F O R M E R
```

ARTISTS
BALLAD
BANJO
BLUEGRASS
CONCERT
COWBOYS
FAITH HILL
FOLK MUSIC
GENRE
GUITARS

HILLBILLY
HONKY TONK
INSTRUMENTS
JOHNNY CASH
LOVE
LYRICS
NASHVILLE
PERFORMER
RADIO
ROCKABILLY

RODEO
ROOTS
ROY ACUFF
SHOWS
SINGERS
SONGS
SOUTHERN
TELEVISION
TENNESSEE

Solution on page 300

The Wizard of Oz

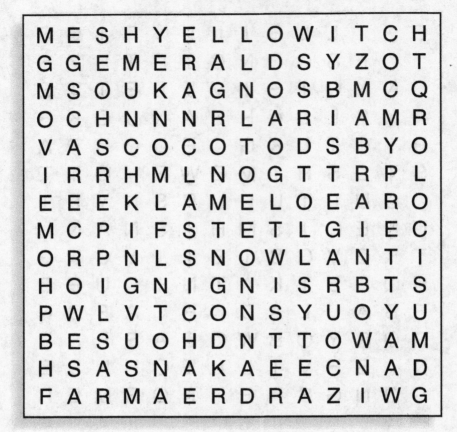

```
M E S H Y E L L O W I T C H
G G E M E R A L D S Y Z O T
M S O U K A G N O S B M C Q
O C H N N N R L A R I A M R
V A S C O C O T O D S B Y O
I R R H M L N O G T T R P L
E E E K L A M E L O E A R O
M C P I F S T E T L G I E C
O R P N L S N O W L A N T I
H O I G N I G N I S R B T S
P W L V T C O N S Y U O Y U
B E S U O H D N T T O W A M
H S A S N A K A E E C N A D
F A R M A E R D R A Z I W G
```

BALLOON	EMERALD	MGM	SHOES
BRAIN	FANTASY	MIDGETS	SINGING
BROOM	FARM	MONKEY	SLIPPERS
CASTLE	GLINDA	MOVIE	SONG
CLASSIC	HEART	MUNCHKIN	TIN
COLOR	HOME	MUSIC	TOTO
COURAGE	HOUSE	MY PRETTY	TWISTER
DANCE	KANSAS	RAINBOW	WITCH
DOG	LION	ROAD	WIZARD
DREAM	LOLLIPOP	SCARECROW	YELLOW

Solution on page 301

Jonas Brothers

```
D N A B Y O B S T A G E I P
C I S U M P O P M K M P R N
S C S L R I G E U O P R A O
O A A N R N R G S O U H T I
U M N T E I E E N O R F I S
N P O O C Y L W T I I G U I
D R J A J O C D J W T R G V
T O N O H K L H S E Y C Y E
R C I W E R C R A C R L A L
A K V U O J O I Y N I S N E
C S E W S L O E N M N R E T
K K K I Y N L N A J G E Y Y
Y D N A M I D F A N S F L L
J G T S M U B L A S M U R D
```

ACTING	GROUP	PURITY RINGS
ALBUMS	GUITAR	SING
AMERICAN	JOE JONAS	SOUNDTRACK
BOY BAND	KEVIN JONAS	STAGE
CAMP ROCK	LYRICS	TAYLOR SWIFT
DISNEY CHANNEL	MANDY	TELEVISION
DRUMS	MILEY CYRUS	TRIO
FAMILY	NEW JERSEY	WHOLESOME
FANS	NICK JONAS	WORLD TOUR
GIRLS	POP MUSIC	

Solution on page 301

Ringling Brothers Circus

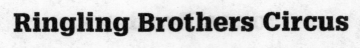

```
F B R O T H E R S C T N E T
K A N W O L C G W O H S M S
C C M M F U N O B M U J O E
I A U I C T E L E P H A N T
R R S B L R I D I A O S K A
C N I I K Y D T R N R E E E
U I C G R N U O V Y S M Y R
S V W T N A A U I D E U S G
T A P O P C O R N O S T T O
E L I P R I N G F G U S U R
K L J O P R I D E S P O N I
C S B Z N E R D L I H C A L
I A C T S M U I D A T S E L
T I G E R A N I M A L S P A
```

ACROBAT	CIRCUS	GOLD TOUR	PEANUTS
ACTS	CLOWN	GORILLA	POPCORN
AMERICAN	COMPANY	GREATEST	RIDES
ANIMALS	COSTUMES	HORSES	RING
AUDIENCE	DOGS	IRVIN FELD	SHOW
BIG TOP	ELEPHANT	JUMBO	STADIUM
BROTHERS	FAMILY	LION	TENT
CARNIVAL	FRANK BUCK	MONKEYS	TICKETS
CHILDREN	FUN	MUSIC	TIGER

Solution on page 301

Toy Story

```
E F R R Y D O O W Y D J Y S
A I D E M G S R R O D T C D
N L B O X E O O L I I O A I
D M V R Q K T L S N P Y R K
Y I R U A S O N I D L S T R
E S E S G B E F E R O P O A
C L S U O Y N T H I T E O X
A I N E C I A R M Y M E N I
P N E G I M D R A L U P O P
S K I T I R F U C B O O K S
Z Y L N T H E A T E R B N K
Z T A W A R D S I S E M A G
U S X L E B X V O I C E S U
B B F Z P X K E N Y K X N K
```

ACTION	CARTOON	KIDS	SID
ALIENS	CGI	MEDIA	SLINKY
ANDY	DINOSAUR	MOVIE	SPACE
ANIMATED	DISNEY	PIXAR	STORY
ARMY MEN	DOLL	PLAY	STUDIOS
AWARDS	FILM	PLOT	THEATER
BARBIE	GAMES	POPULAR	TOYS
BO PEEP	HIT	REX	TRILOGY
BOOKS	INFINITY	SEQUEL	VOICES
BUZZ	KEN	SERIES	WOODY

Solution on page 301

Tron

```
N N Y L F F R A N C H I S E L
L M H D E E M A R F N I A M
D A F T P U N K I E M S T J
V R I N C C Q C L U L O E S
R G I R O Y T E L C I F C E
E O H F O I C A S E F T H C
T R A U O T T Y D B G W N U
U P C N R I A A R A R A O R
P S K O O B C I M O C R L I
M R N N M R D E D I T E O T
O I O O A G N I R A N S G Y
C K V T E I R E S A L A Y M
N I J S C G M L A T I G I D
E P T G R A P H I C S I D P
```

ACTOR	DIGITAL	GAME	PROGRAM
AMERICAN	DISC	GLADIATORIAL	SECURITY
ANIMATION	ELECTRONIC	GRAPHICS	SEQUEL
ARCADE	ENCOM	GRID	SIMULATION
CINEMA	FICTION	HACK	SOFTWARE
CLU	FILM	JEFF BRIDGES	STORY
COMIC BOOKS	FLYNN	LASER	TECHNOLOGY
COMPUTER	FRANCHISE	MAINFRAME	YORI
DAFT PUNK	FUN	MOVIE	

Solution on page 302

Super Mario

```
Y A L P E A C H R E S C U E
W R E P U S P I P E A M B M
O I R A W Z I E V S P O M A
R Z R R U W Z I T M O D U G
L S L E V E L L U G O G S R
D M Q W T F E J E U K N I A
I A T O O R C L A S S I C T
H S V L I T A L I A N K O S
S C E F R G R U A O R A N C
O O D I A Z T A Q U D R S O
Y T A G M P O I N T S T O I
T O C I R E O E D I V U L N
Y V R U F U N S L E U Q E S
G O A L S E R E S W O B T M
```

ARCADE	GAME	MARIO	RUN
BOWSER	GOALS	MASCOT	SEQUELS
CARTOON	ITALIAN	MUSIC	STAR
CASTLE	JUMP	PEACH	SUPER
CLASSIC	KART	PIPE	TOAD
COINS	KINGDOM	PLAY	VIDEO
CONSOLE	KOOPA	POINTS	WARIO
ENEMIES	LEVELS	PUZZLES	WII
FLOWER	LIVES	QUARTER	WORLD
FUN	LUIGI	RESCUE	YOSHI

Solution on page 302

Phonograph

```
G N I W S T S O N G S Y R G
E N R T U R N T A B L E E U
I L I R E K A E P S C K D D
O N D Y B X C S T O N C N L
I R G E A N U A R A N O I O
D O E W E L J D R I P J L U
A H S I Y N P C P V M C Y D
R I C T P L A S T I C S C A
M S S O A I N V E N T I O N
W T P Y A U D I O T U D E C
G O E N O H P O M A R G S I
I R E C O R D I N G S I I N
B Y A L B U M S T E R E O G
M U S E U M S O U N D S N L
```

ALBUMS	HORN	PLAYING	SPIN
ARM	INVENTION	RADIO	STEREO
AUDIO	LOUD	RCA	STYLUS
BIG	LPS	RECORD PLAYER	SWING
CRANK	MUSEUM	RECORDINGS	TURNTABLE
CYLINDER	NEEDLE	RIDGES	VINTAGE
DANCING	NOISE	SCIENCE	WAX
DISC JOCKEY	OLD	SONGS	
GRAMOPHONE	PATENT	SOUNDS	
HISTORY	PLASTIC	SPEAKER	

Solution on page 302

I Want My MTV

```
D S D R A W A C I S U M K E
J V G A R T I S T S H C I R
T I E N C T S S N D O I N O
I D L R O W L A E R E H T H
M E B K U S X K M A P L E S
E O A R N L R C N W O E R Y
S J C O T L V A I A P N V E
S O T Y D I J J A E U N I S
Q C S W O H S Y T I L A E R
U K O E W E D I R V A H W E
A E H N N H N C E O R C S J
R Y N E E T A D T M E D I A
E S K A E R B G N I R P S D
M U S I C V I D E O S F T O
```

ARTISTS	JACKASS	ROCK
BANDS	JERSEY SHORE	SONGS
CABLE	MEDIA	SPRING BREAK
CHANNEL	MOVIE AWARDS	TEEN
COUNTDOWN	MUSIC AWARDS	THE HILLS
ENTERTAINMENT	MUSIC VIDEOS	THE REAL WORLD
HITS	NEW YORK	TIMES SQUARE
HOST	POPULAR	VIDEO JOCKEYS
INTERVIEWS	REALITY SHOWS	VJS

Solution on page 302

Salsa Music

```
J D C L U B S T E P M U R T
O N Z Z A J Q L S O G N O B
H U R N G C M I M A O H M B
N O D E N O U S U P B K A Q
N S T W I N S T R U M E N T
Y U F Y S G I E D E A V T S
P O P O D A C N G R M O I P
A C I R E M A N I T A L C A
C I A K T R O M B O N E L N
H X N O I S S U C R E P S I
E E O U T S P I C I N E S S
C M N A F F G N I C N A D H
O J E R N E G C M O D E R N
Q B S T Y L E O G N A T R A
```

ART	GENRE	MEXICO	SONG
BANDS	HOT	MODERN	SOUND
BEATS	INSTRUMENT	MUSIC	SPANISH
BONGOS	JAZZ	NEW YORK	SPICINESS
CLUBS	JOHNNY PACHECO	PERCUSSION	STYLE
CONGA	LATIN AMERICA	PIANO	TANGO
DANCING	LISTEN	PUERTO RICO	TROMBONE
DRUMS	LOVE	ROMANTIC	TRUMPET
FUN	MAMBO	SING	

Solution on page 303

Nirvana

```
P L Y R I C S E A T T L E A
D Y B R I M C H E R E N R R
R E A Y U N P L U G G E D A
O N N R E O B K A Z N A F T
C T D I L V T T Z K N U P I
E R D V O O S U C O X D R U
R U H T H S B O I I D R E G
A O C M A E R T S N I A M Y
L C A B V L C S U B P O O V
U O E O M I E O M L J B T O
P B L R D C S G R O H L I C
O A B D C V I D E O S L O A
P I A U T G R A M M Y I N L
H N S A L B U M P O P B U S
```

ADDICTION	EMOTION	LOVE BUZZ	SEATTLE
ALBUM	ERA	LYRICS	SOUND
AUDIENCE	FAN	MAINSTREAM	STAGE
BAND	GRAMMY	MTV	SUB POP
BASS	GROHL	MUSIC	SUCCESS
BILLBOARD	GRUNGE	NOVOSELIC	TOUR
BLEACH	GUITAR	POPULAR	UNPLUGGED
COBAIN	HOLE	PUNK	VIDEOS
COURTNEY	IN BLOOM	RECORD	VOCALS
DRUMS	KURT	ROCK	

Solution on page 303

Listen to the Radio

```
R S A H O S T A M R O F K Z
A T L N D K M E U W D L L D
G S A P T R R P R J A I A N
G E N R A E F O S O N V T E
D T G D L N N P W T C E E W
W N I N T E R N E T E K P S
M O S B C T N R A O E R J D
U C I Y S S L N S P O N E L
S S U D T I P U A G L D C O
I W A L A L I U R H E N B C
C O U N T R Y A B E C A A D
B H D A I U M Z R L N R W I
L S I S O J R F A D I B L A
I S O U N D O E S N E C I L
```

ABC	COUNTRY	LISTEN	PUBLIC
AM RADIO	CULTURE	LIVE	ROCK
ANTENNA	DANCE	MUSIC	SHOWS
AUDIO	DIAL	NBC	SIGNAL
BANDS	FM RADIO	NETWORK	SIRIUS
BRAND	FORMAT	NEWS	SOUND
CAR	FREE	NPR	STATION
CBS	HOST	OLD	STEREO
CHANNEL	INTERNET	POP	TALK
CONTESTS	LICENSE	PROGRAM	WAVES

Solution on page 303

Margaritaville

```
F C F L O R I D A L B U M S
Y T I R A H C O U N T R Y O
N R N S O N G W R I T E R I
M O S Y U H D K A R T I S T
M P I N A M S S E N I S U B
U I E T C D H T D Y K F H T
S C A R A A N C R N W C S O
I A X M F C R O A E A E O U
C L O N I O A I M E C L S R
I A U T H O R V B E B N S T
A F A L A B A M A B M A O I
N A S H V I L L E N E O N C
T N A R U A T S E R H A C D
Y S U N P A R A D I S E N J
```

ALABAMA	COUNTRY	PALM BEACH
ALBUMS	FANS	PARADISE
ARTIST	FINS	PERFORMER
AUTHOR	FLORIDA	RESTAURANT
BAND	FUN	ROCK
BEACH MUSIC	HOOT	SONGWRITER
BUSINESSMAN	ISLANDS	SUN
CARIBBEAN	KEY WEST	TOUR
CHARITY	MIAMI	TROPICAL
COME MONDAY	MUSICIAN	VACATION
CONCERTS	NASHVILLE	

Solution on page 303

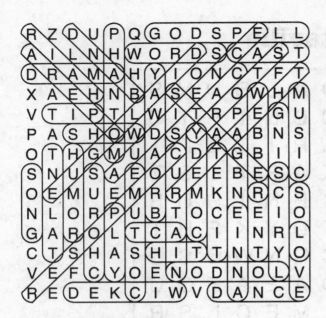

CHAPTER 1: Musical Theater

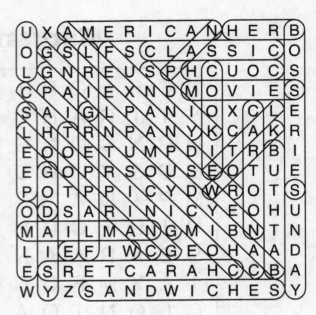

CHAPTER 1: Blondie Comics

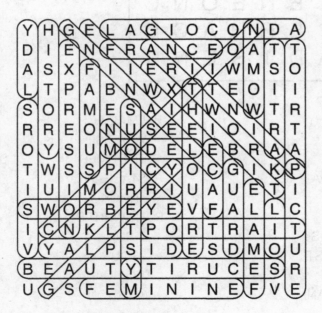

CHAPTER 1: *The Mona Lisa*

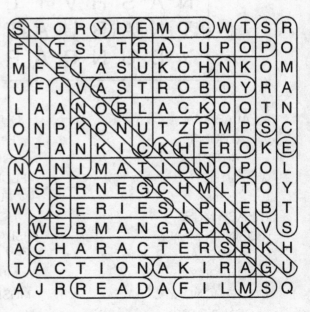

CHAPTER 1: Manga Art

CHAPTER 1: **Arts and Crafts**

CHAPTER 1: **American Folklore**

CHAPTER 1: **Ancient Egyptian Hieroglyphs**

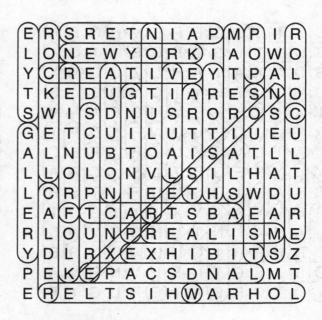

CHAPTER 1: **Art in America**

CHAPTER 1: Dance in the United States

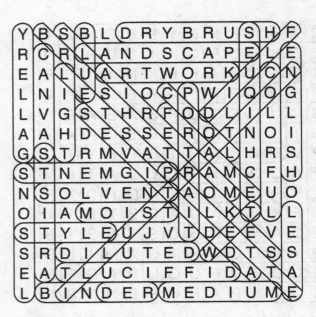

CHAPTER 1: Painting Art

CHAPTER 1: Sculpture

CHAPTER 1: Hey, It's the Monkees!

CHAPTER 1: Tom Sawyer

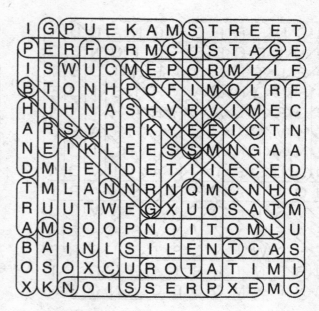

CHAPTER 1: Mime Artists

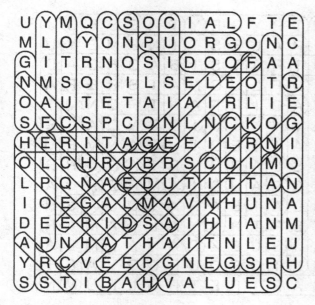

CHAPTER 1: Culture

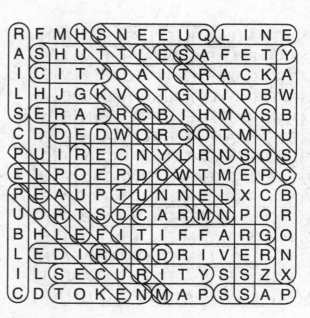

CHAPTER 2: New York City Subway

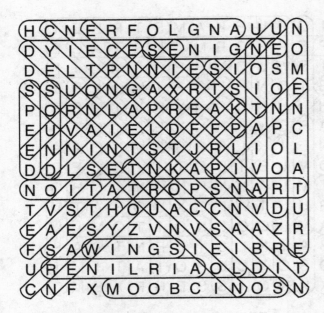

CHAPTER 2: Flying the Concorde

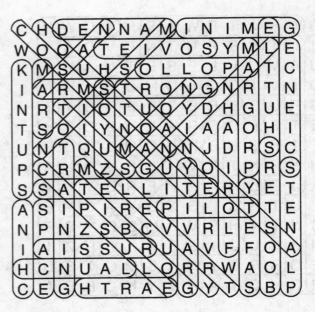

CHAPTER 2: Traveling in Space

CHAPTER 2: Seaplane

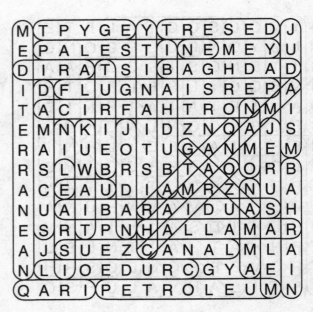

CHAPTER 2: Around the Middle East

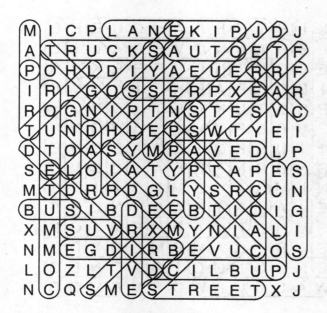

CHAPTER 2: On the Highway

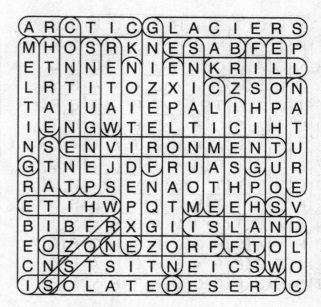

CHAPTER 2: Antarctica Tour

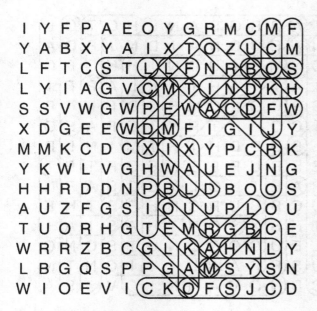

CHAPTER 2: Airport Letters

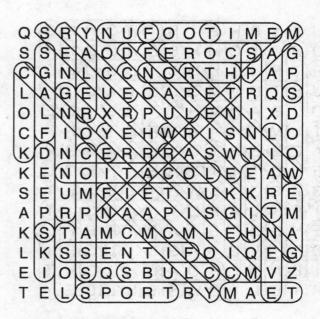

CHAPTER 2: Orienteering

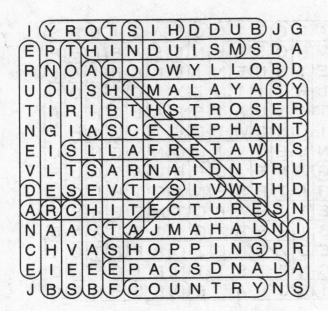

CHAPTER 2: See India

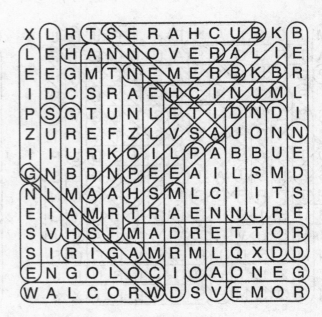

CHAPTER 2: Cities of Europe

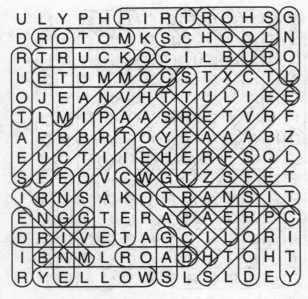

CHAPTER 2: Take the Bus

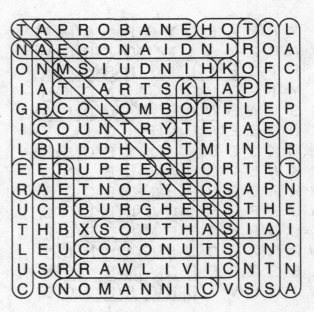

CHAPTER 2: Visit Sri Lanka

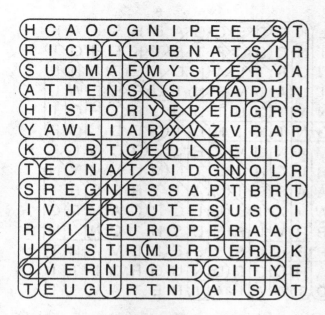

CHAPTER 2: Aboard the Orient Express

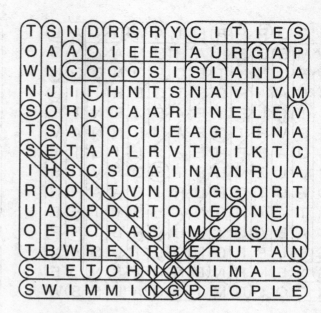

CHAPTER 2: Costa Rica Trip

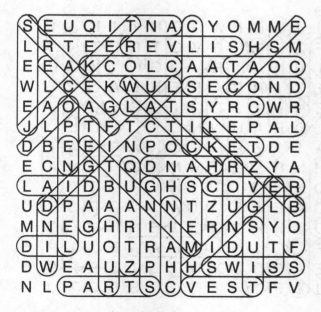

CHAPTER 3: Pocket Watch

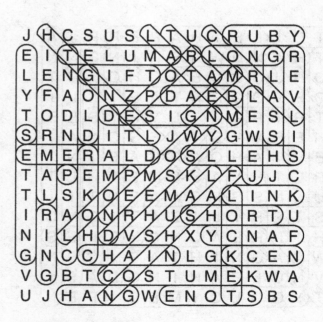

CHAPTER 3: Necklaces

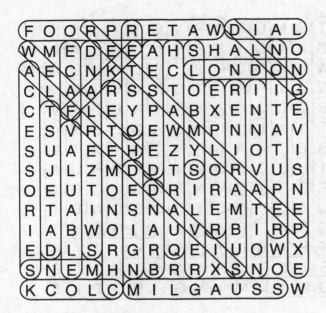

CHAPTER 3: My Rolex

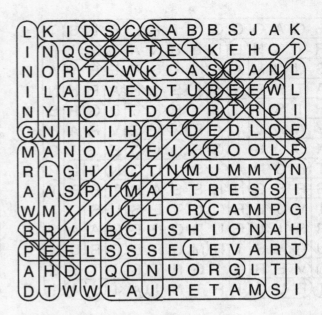

CHAPTER 3: Sleeping Bag

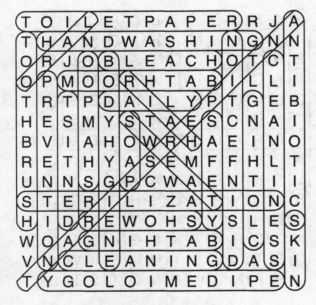

CHAPTER 3: Personal Hygiene

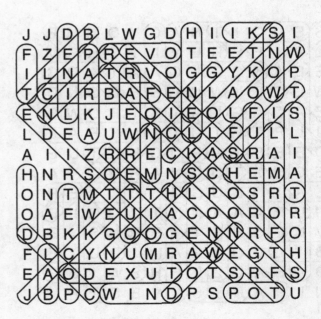

CHAPTER 3: Put on a Coat

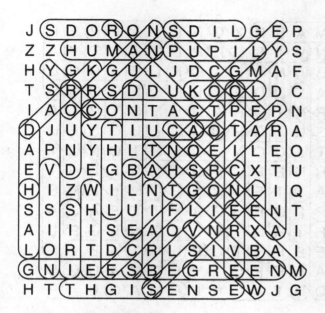

CHAPTER 3: Our Eyes

CHAPTER 3: Things to Wear

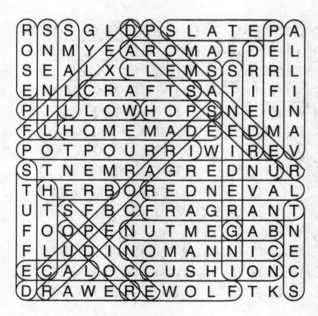

CHAPTER 3: Sachet

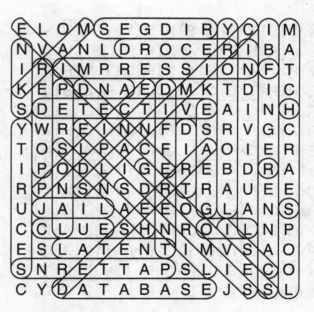

CHAPTER 3: Leaving Fingerprints

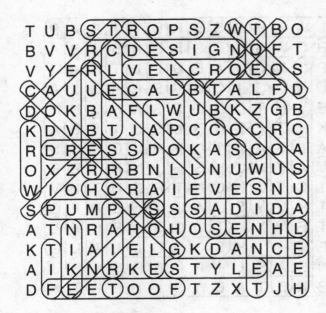

CHAPTER 3: Your Shoes

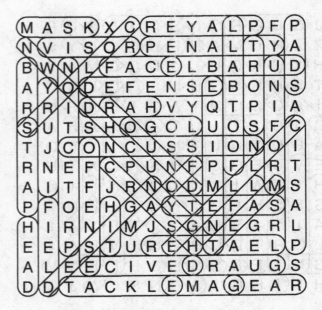

CHAPTER 3: Football Helmet

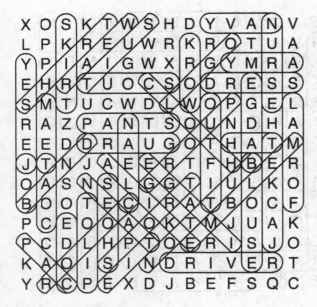

CHAPTER 3: Uniforms

CHAPTER 3: Bracelets

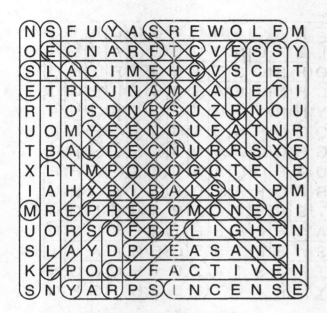

CHAPTER 3: Wearing Perfume

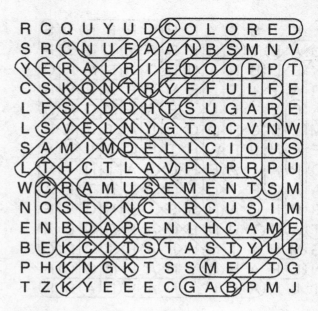

CHAPTER 4: Cotton Candy

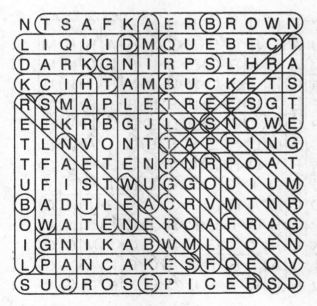

CHAPTER 4: Sweet Maple Syrup

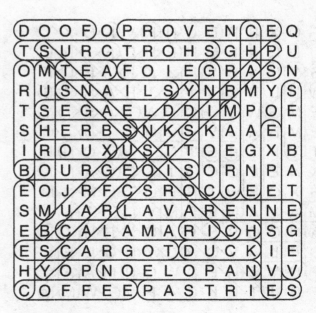

CHAPTER 4: French Food

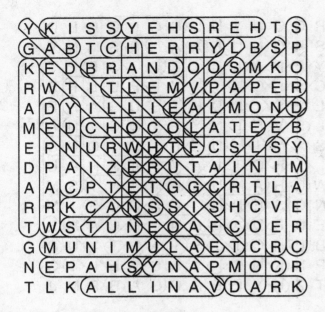

CHAPTER 4: Hershey's Kisses

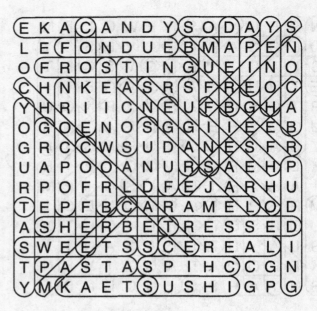

CHAPTER 4: Yummy Things

CHAPTER 4: Hot Chocolate

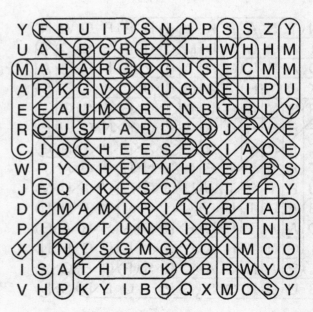

CHAPTER 4: Cheesecake, Please

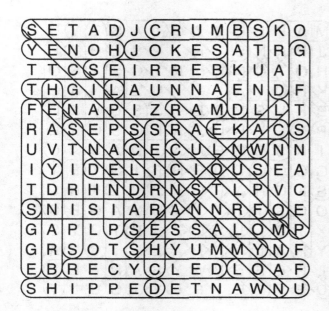

CHAPTER 4: Fruitcakes

CHAPTER 4: Berry Good

CHAPTER 4: Pizza Toppings

CHAPTER 4: Fondue

CHAPTER 4: Going Bananas

CHAPTER 4: Bacon

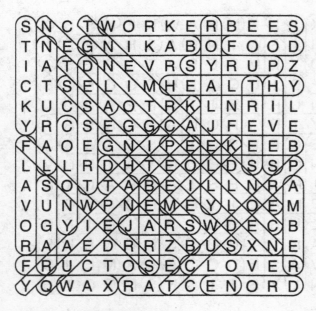

CHAPTER 4: Sticky Honey

CHAPTER 4: Coke

CHAPTER 5: Words with an AM

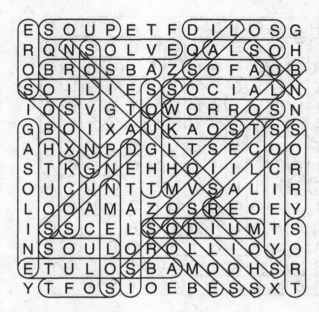

CHAPTER 5: Words with a SO

CHAPTER 5: Words That End with *K*

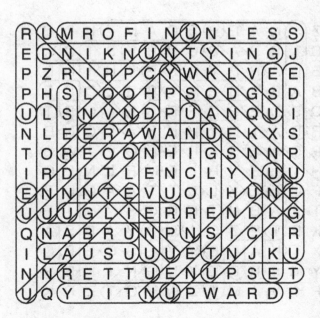

CHAPTER 5: Words That Begin with *U*

CHAPTER 5: Words That End with *C*

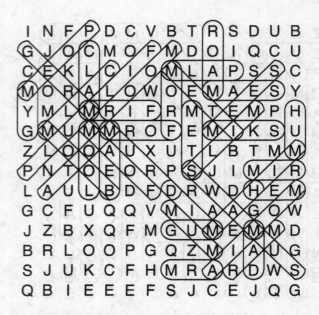

CHAPTER 5: Words That End with *M*

CHAPTER 5: Words with a BE

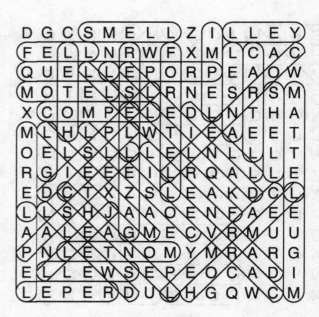

CHAPTER 5: Rhymes with Belle

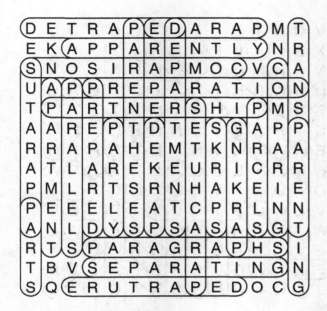

CHAPTER 5: Words on PAR

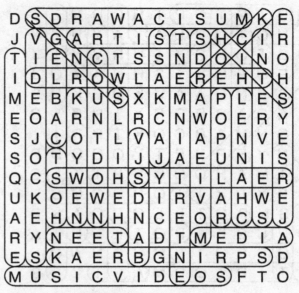

CHAPTER 5: Words with *Es*

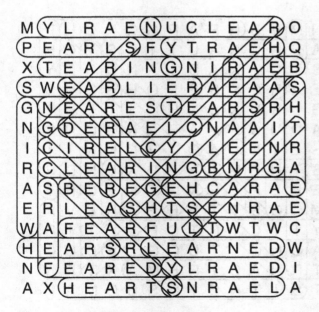

CHAPTER 5: Words with an EAR

CHAPTER 5: Words That Begin with *F*

CHAPTER 5: Words with TOP

CHAPTER 5: Rhymes with Sue

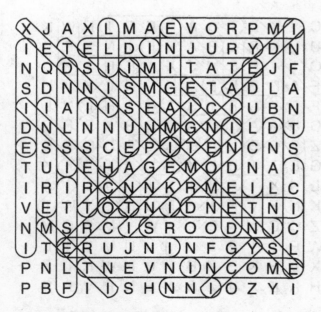

CHAPTER 5: Words That Begin with *I*

CHAPTER 6: Alexander Graham Bell

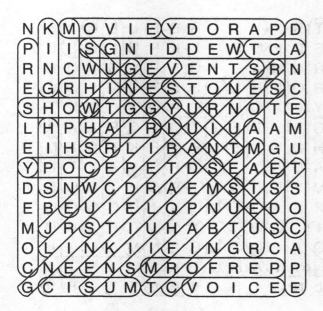

CHAPTER 6: Elvis Impersonators

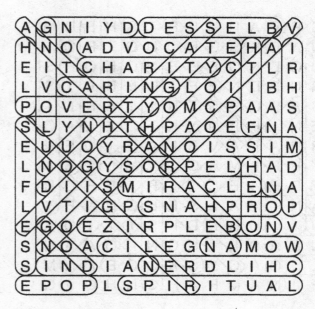

CHAPTER 6: Mother Teresa

CHAPTER 6: Al Capone

CHAPTER 6: Audrey Hepburn

CHAPTER 6: Johnny Appleseed

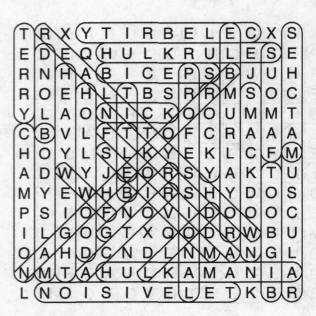

CHAPTER 6: Hulk Hogan

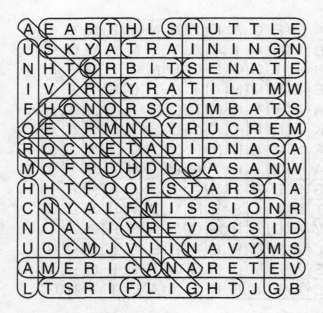

CHAPTER 6: John Glenn

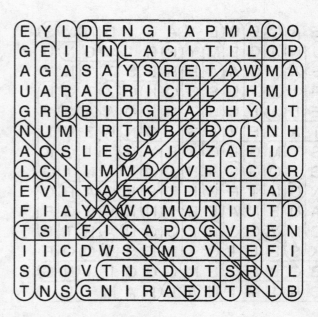

CHAPTER 6: Helen Keller

CHAPTER 6: Oprah

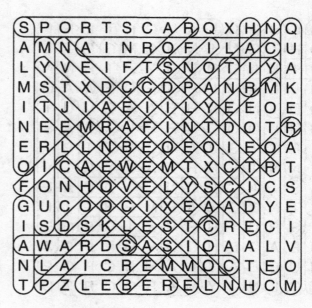

CHAPTER 6: James Dean

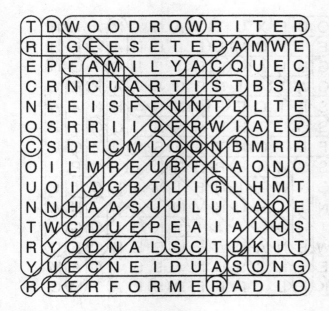

CHAPTER 6: Woody Guthrie

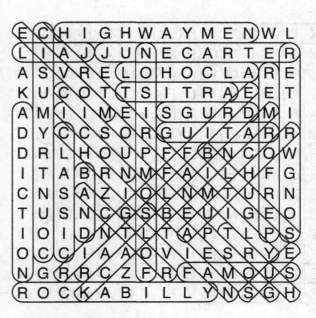

CHAPTER 6: Johnny Cash

CHAPTER 6: Captain Kangaroo

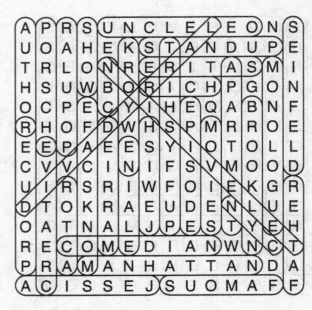

CHAPTER 6: Jerry Seinfeld

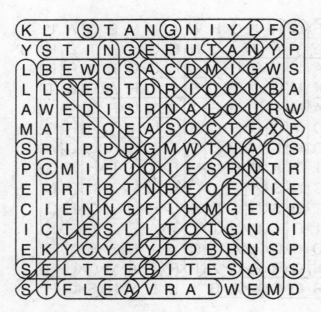

CHAPTER 7: Insect Life

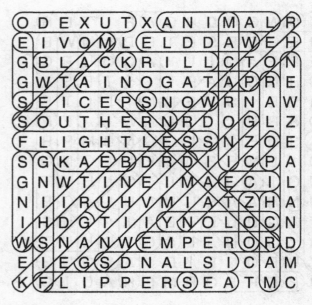

CHAPTER 7: Penguins Are Birds

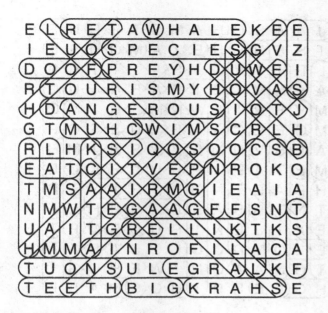

CHAPTER 7: Great White Shark

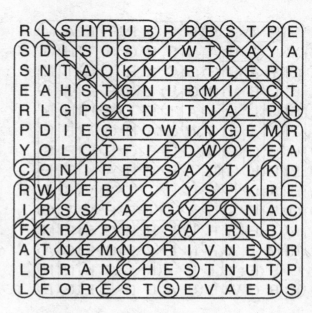

CHAPTER 7: Amazing Trees

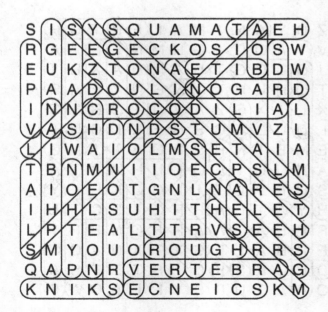

CHAPTER 7: Cold Blood

CHAPTER 7: Dachshunds

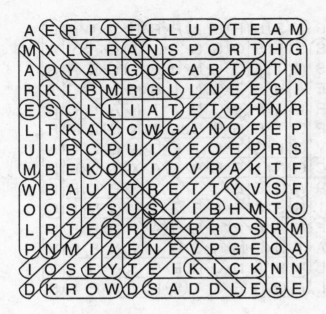

CHAPTER 7: Mules

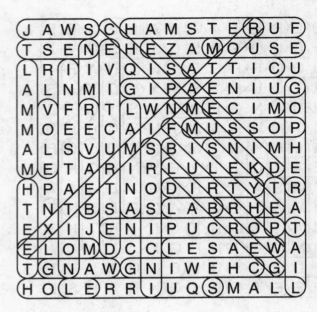

CHAPTER 7: Rodents

CHAPTER 7: Eagles

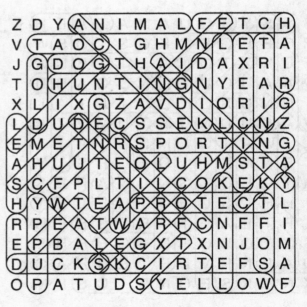

CHAPTER 7: Golden Retriever

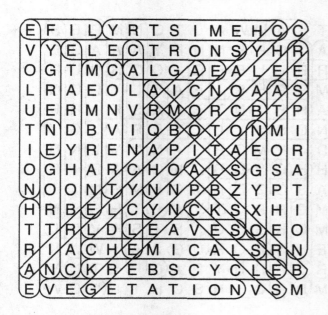

CHAPTER 7: **Photosynthesis**

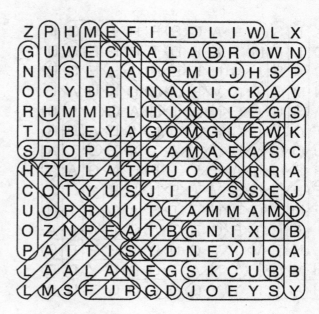

CHAPTER 7: **Kangaroos**

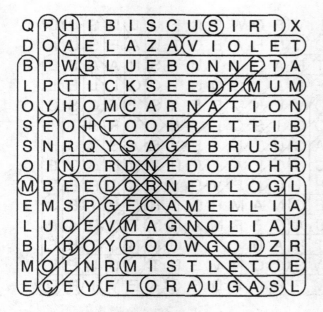

CHAPTER 7: **All Kinds of Flowers**

CHAPTER 7: **Organic Food**

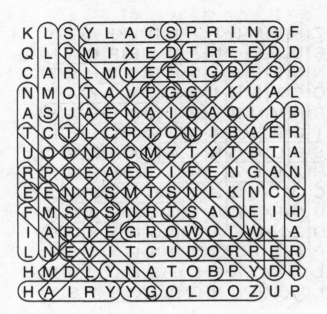

CHAPTER 7: Buds

CHAPTER 8: Business People

CHAPTER 8: Nike, Inc.

CHAPTER 8: Buy a Mercedes

CHAPTER 8: *The Wall Street Journal*

CHAPTER 8: **Currency Around the World**

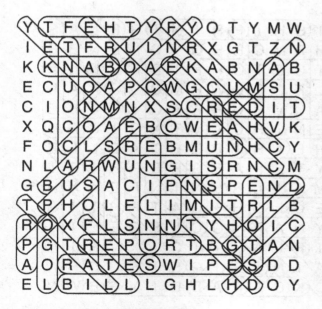

CHAPTER 8: **Credit Cards**

CHAPTER 8: **Bill Gates**

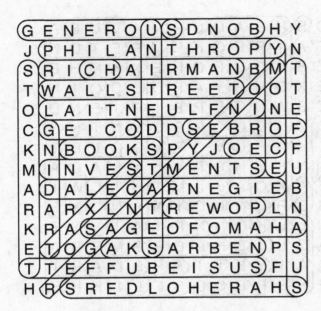

CHAPTER 8: Warren Buffett

CHAPTER 8: Delivery Service

CHAPTER 8: MGM

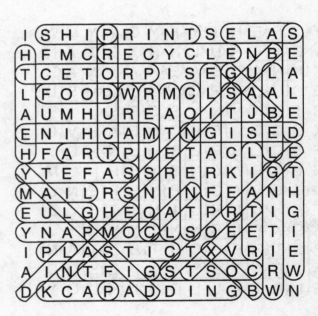

CHAPTER 8: Packaging

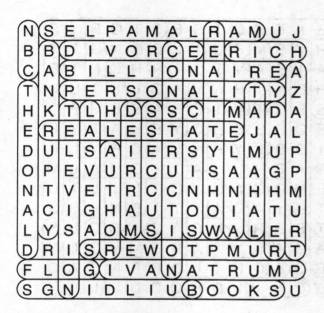

CHAPTER 8: Donald Trump

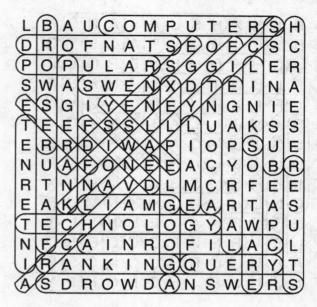

CHAPTER 8: Google Inc.

CHAPTER 8: Business Trade

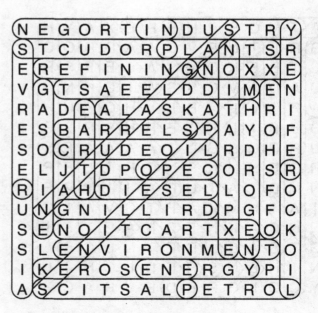

CHAPTER 8: The Petroleum Business

CHAPTER 9: Door Handles

CHAPTER 9: Toy Shelf

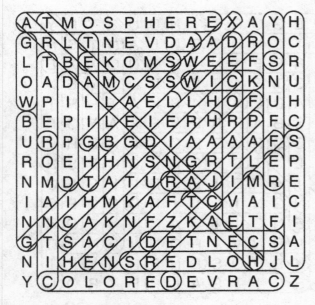

CHAPTER 9: Light a Candle

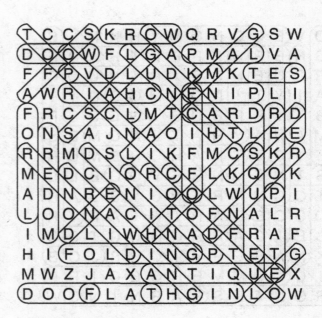

CHAPTER 9: Tables

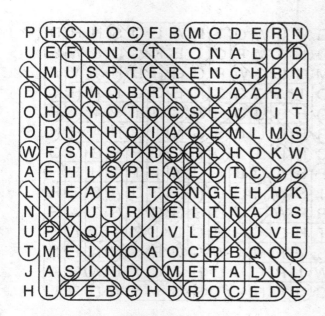

CHAPTER 9: Move the Furniture

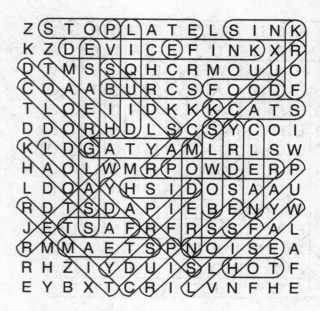

CHAPTER 9: Dishwasher

CHAPTER 9: Interior Design

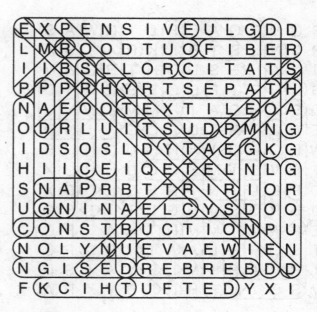

CHAPTER 9: Carpets

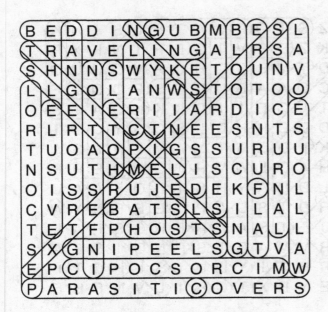

CHAPTER 9: Bedbugs Are Here

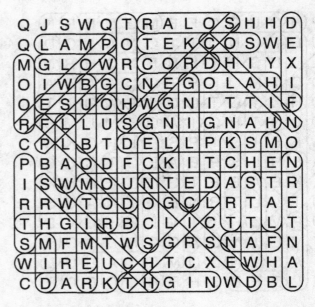

CHAPTER 9: Light Fixtures

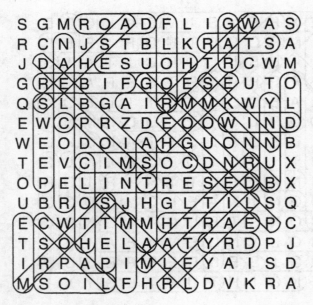

CHAPTER 9: Dust

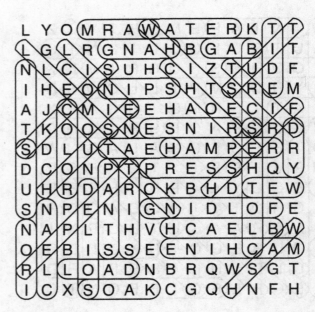

CHAPTER 9: Laundry

CHAPTER 9: **Bed**

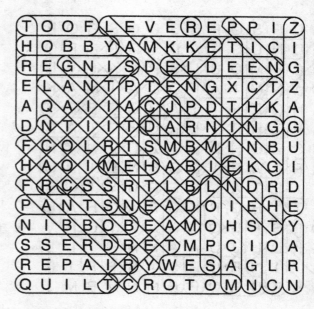

CHAPTER 9: **Sewing Machine**

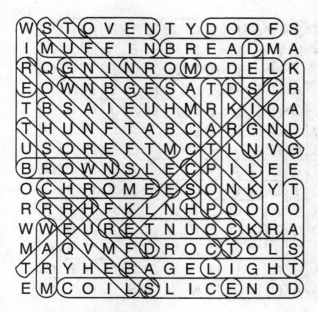

CHAPTER 9: **Toaster**

CHAPTER 10: **Amusement Arcade**

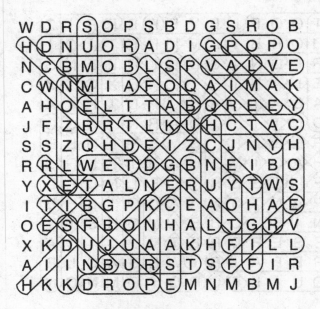

CHAPTER 10: Water Balloons

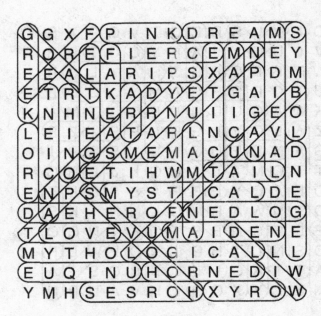

CHAPTER 10: Fabled Unicorns

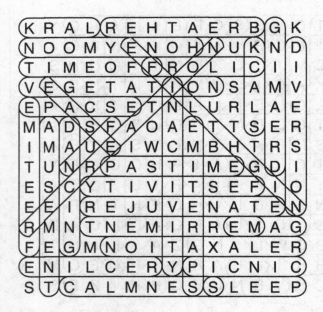

CHAPTER 10: Leisure

CHAPTER 10: Spring Break Time

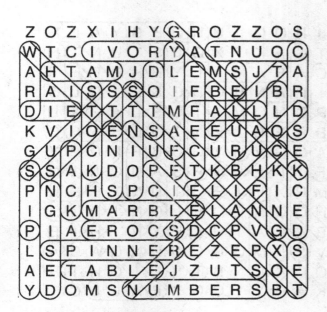

CHAPTER 10: Dominoes

CHAPTER 10: Funfair

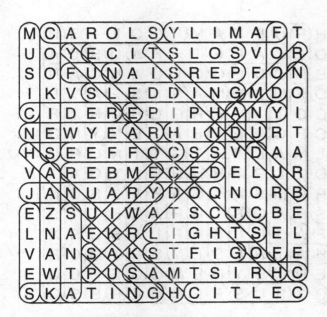

CHAPTER 10: Winter Celebrations

CHAPTER 10: Waterslide

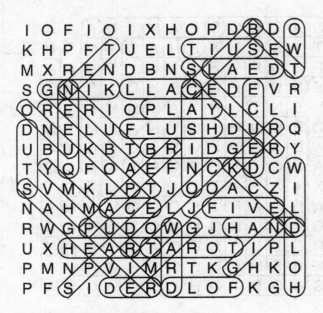

CHAPTER 10: **Play Cards**

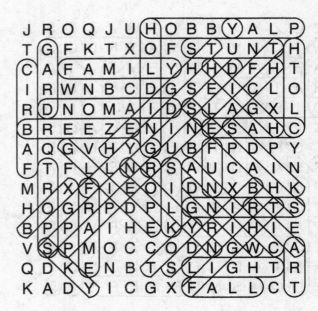

CHAPTER 10: **Kites**

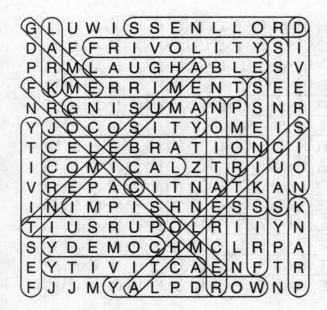

CHAPTER 10: **Fun Fun Fun**

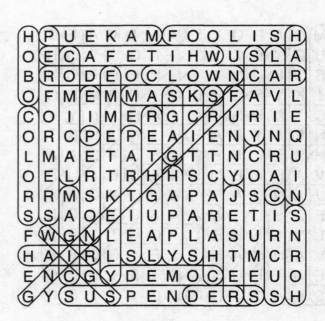

CHAPTER 10: **Clowns**

284

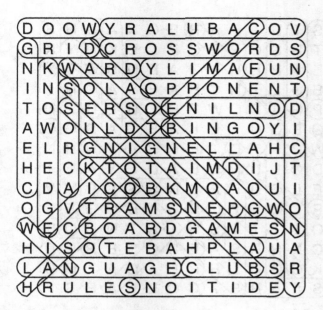

CHAPTER 10: Let's Play Scrabble

CHAPTER 10: It's a Picnic

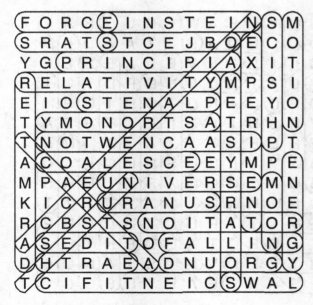

CHAPTER 11: The Law of Gravity

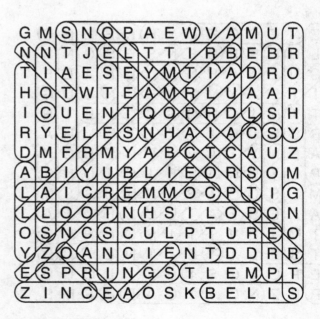

CHAPTER 11: Bronze

CHAPTER 11: Aurora

CHAPTER 11: Avalanche

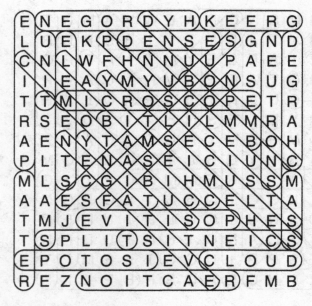

CHAPTER 11: Atoms

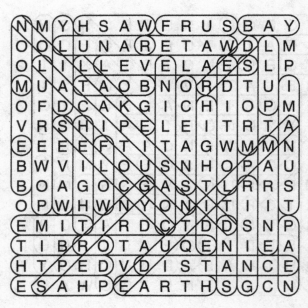

CHAPTER 11: Tidal

CHAPTER 11: Mining the Earth

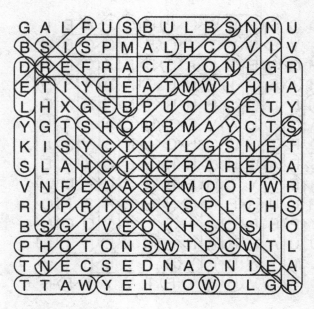

CHAPTER 11: Light

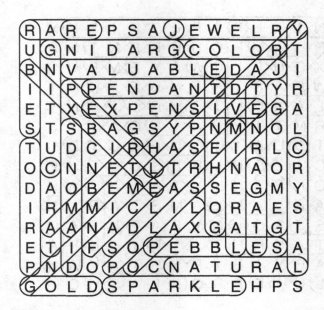

CHAPTER 11: Gemstone

CHAPTER 11: Natural Gas

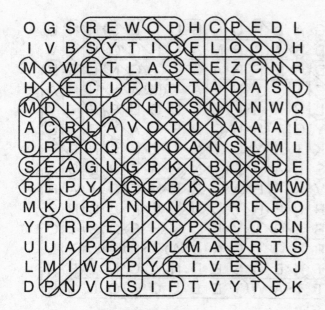

CHAPTER 11: Water Resources

CHAPTER 11: Quantum Theory

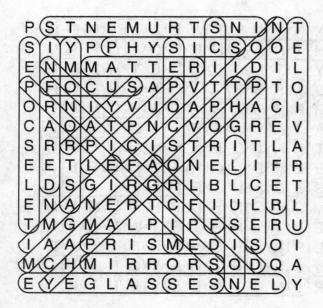

CHAPTER 11: Optics

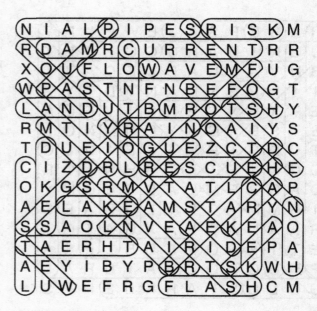

CHAPTER 11: Floods

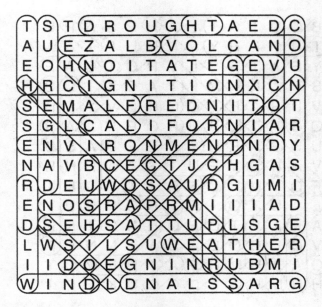

CHAPTER 11: Like Wildfire

CHAPTER 12: Fencing

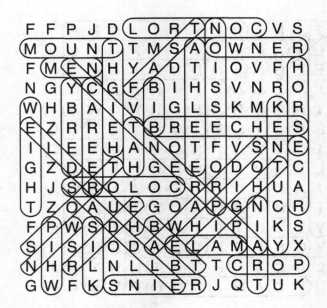

CHAPTER 12: Jockey

CHAPTER 12: Snowboard

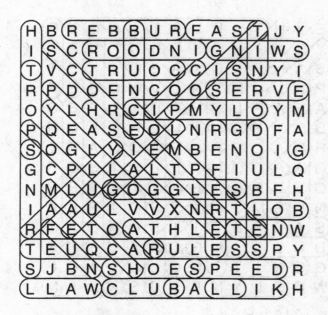

CHAPTER 12: Squash

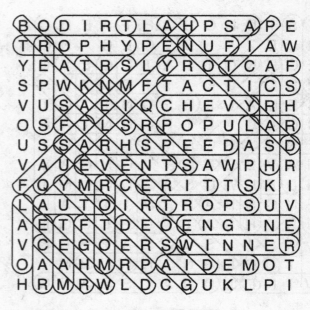

CHAPTER 12: Stock Car Racing

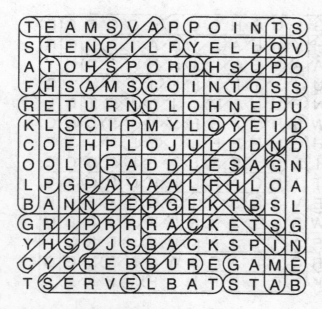

CHAPTER 12: Table Tennis

CHAPTER 12: Synchronized Swimming

CHAPTER 12: Miniature Golf

CHAPTER 12: Wrestling

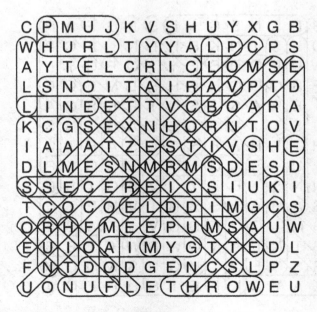

CHAPTER 12: Dodgeball

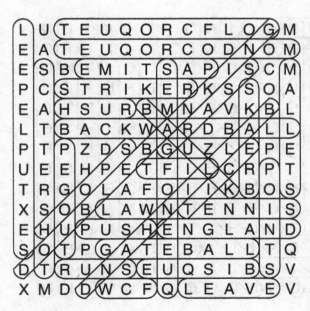

CHAPTER 12: Croquet

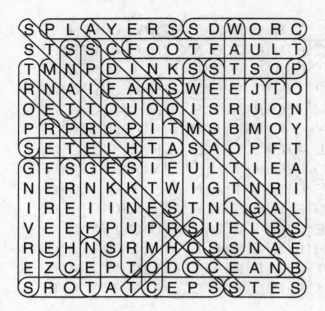

CHAPTER 12: **Beach Volleyball**

CHAPTER 12: **Little League Baseball**

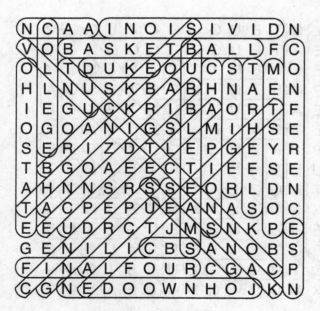

CHAPTER 12: **Basketball Madness**

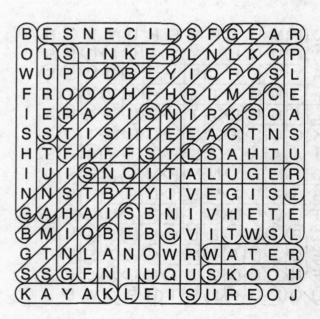

CHAPTER 12: **Fishing**

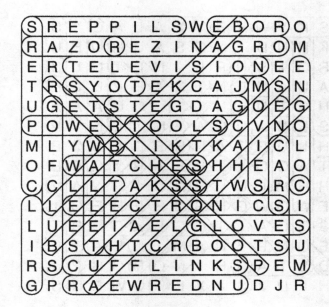

CHAPTER 13: Things for Him

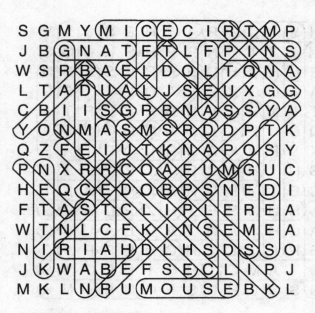

CHAPTER 13: Little Things

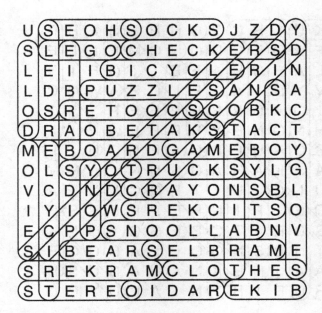

CHAPTER 13: Things for Kids

CHAPTER 13: Things That Crawl

CHAPTER 13: Red Things

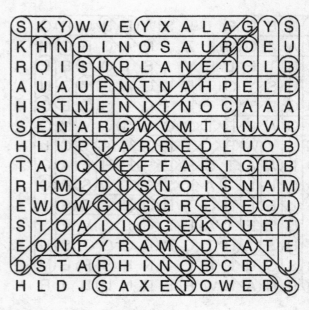

CHAPTER 13: Big Things

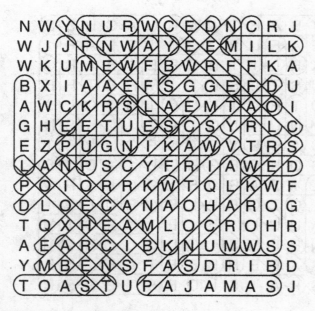

CHAPTER 13: Morning Things

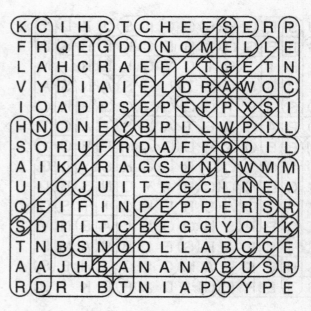

CHAPTER 13: Yellow Things

CHAPTER 13: Things for Her

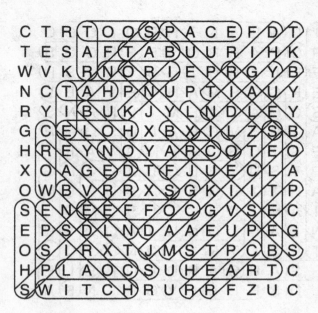

CHAPTER 13: Black Things

CHAPTER 13: Things on Wheels

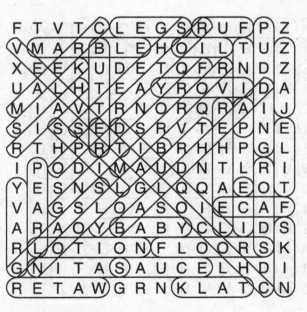

CHAPTER 13: Smooth Things

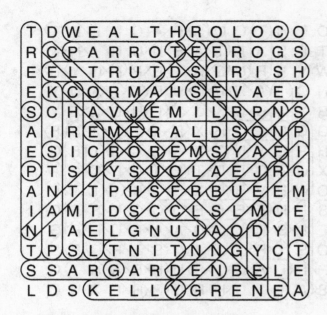

CHAPTER 13: Things That Are Green

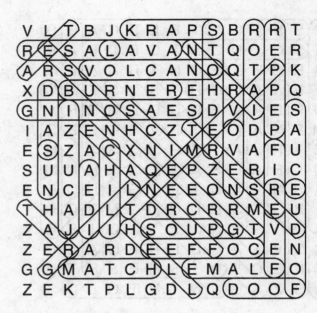

CHAPTER 13: Hot Things

CHAPTER 13: Cold Things

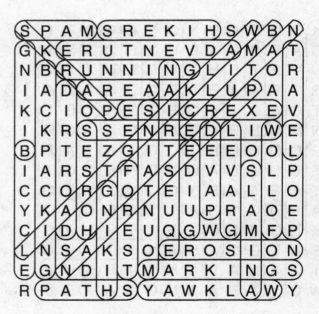

CHAPTER 14: Hit the Trail

CHAPTER 14: **Utility Poles**

CHAPTER 14: **Dunes**

CHAPTER 14: **Australia's Great Barrier Reef**

CHAPTER 14: **Niagara Falls**

CHAPTER 14: **Bird Feeders**

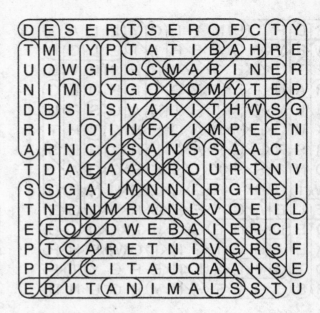

CHAPTER 14: **Ecosystem**

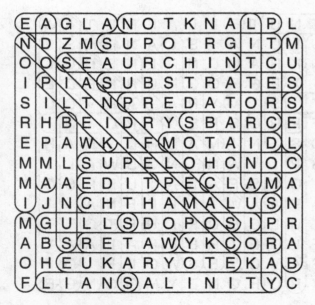

CHAPTER 14: **Intertidal**

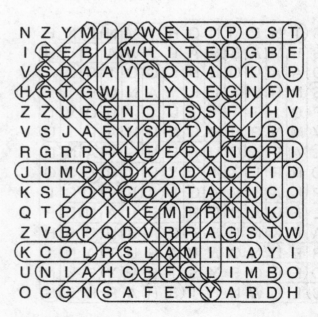

CHAPTER 14: **Fence**

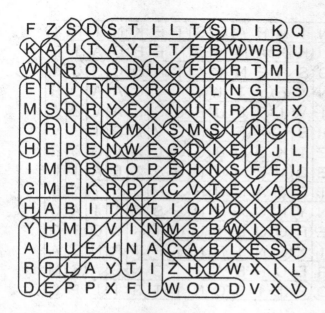

CHAPTER 14: Tree House

CHAPTER 14: Mount Everest

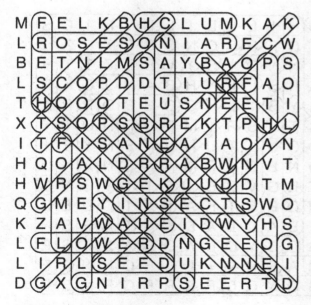

CHAPTER 14: Garden

CHAPTER 14: Kelp Forest

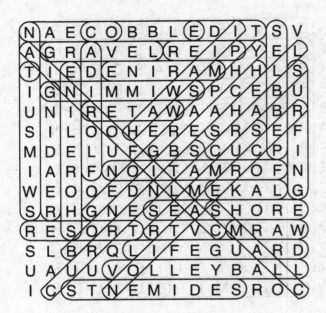

CHAPTER 14: Around the Beach

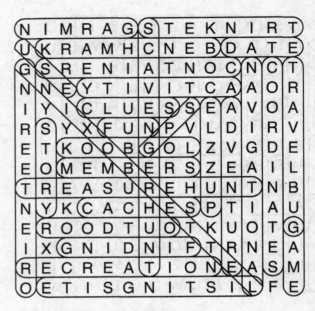

CHAPTER 14: Geocaching Fun

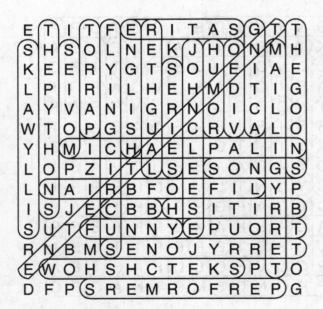

CHAPTER 15: Monty Python

CHAPTER 15: Country Music

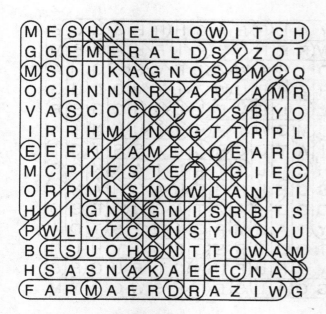

CHAPTER 15: *The Wizard of Oz*

CHAPTER 15: Jonas Brothers

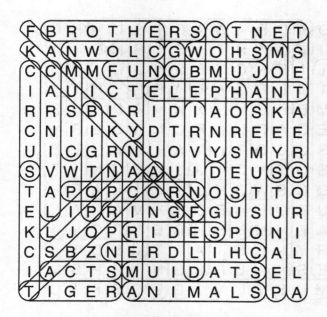

CHAPTER 15: Ringling Brothers Circus

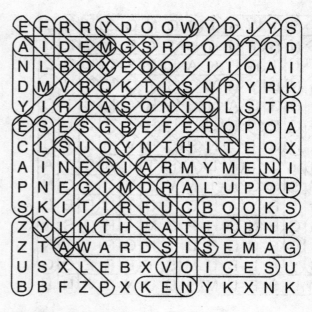

CHAPTER 15: *Toy Story*

CHAPTER 15: *Tron*

CHAPTER 15: Super Mario

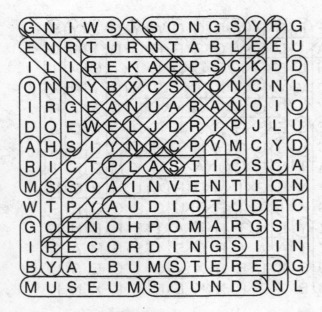

CHAPTER 15: Phonograph

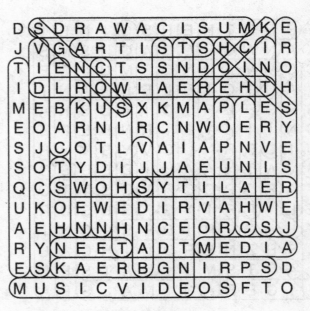

CHAPTER 15: I Want My MTV

CHAPTER 15: Salsa Music

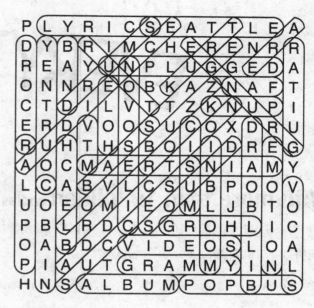

CHAPTER 15: Nirvana

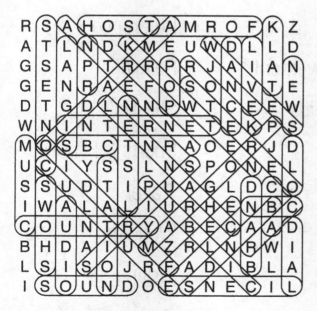

CHAPTER 15: Listen to the Radio

CHAPTER 15: Margaritaville

We Have

EVERYTHING®

on Anything!

The Everything® list spans a wide range of subjects, with more than 500 titles covering 25 different categories:

Business	History	Reference
Careers	Home Improvement	Religion
Children's Storybooks	Everything Kids	Self-Help
Computers	Languages	Sports & Fitness
Cooking	Music	Travel
Crafts and Hobbies	New Age	Wedding
Education/Schools	Parenting	Writing
Games and Puzzles	Personal Finance	
Health	Pets